WOMEN AND THE LAKES

UNTOLD GREAT LAKES MARITIME TALES

FREDERICK STONEHOUSE

AVERY COLOR STUDIOS, INC.
GWINN, MICHIGAN

©2001 Avery Color Studios, Inc.

ISBN 1-892384-10-8

Library of Congress Control Number: 2001087136

First Edition 2001

Published by
Avery Color Studios, Inc.
Gwinn, Michigan 49841

TABLE OF CONTENTS

FOREWORD

Women And The Lakes is largely anecdotal history. It looks at events only narrowly and does not seek to evaluate them against a measurable criteria. But, being anecdotal, it celebrates the triumph and tragedy of the individual rather than of the faceless masses.

From the beginning of lakes navigation until comparatively recently, women were generally not employed in the maritime trades. Traditionally the menfolk earned the living and women kept house. But then the practical side of things often intervened. Husbands and fathers died and then women had to earn a living, to provide for themselves and their families. They had to find employment. In the maritime trades their opportunities were very limited, that of ship's cook being the most common. But there were exceptions, those that served as inspiration for others. And that is what *Women And The Lakes* is about.

It is often alleged that behind every good man there's a good woman; or maybe even a better woman. Great Lakes history as history has long been the domain of men. They were the explorers, voyagers and missionaries who mapped the new lands. They lived among the Indians, built the towns and captained the ships, manned the lighthouses and salvaged the wrecks. The popular history of the

Women often were an important part of Great Lakes fishing operations. Lake Superior Maritime Museum.

1

Great Lakes is the story of these men and what they accomplished. Women were there only in the shadows.

But interspersed through the whole fabric of Great Lakes history are the women, mostly forgotten if not unknown, who contributed so much to the history of the lakes. It was the women who kept house at the lighthouse and maintained the home fires while their husbands sailed the lakes. They did the myriad of things, large and small, necessary to hold the families together. The work was not glamorous, and it usually wasn't paid and often unrecognized, but it was as important as that of the husbands.

To be complete, the maritime history of the Great Lakes must include all of the participants, male and female. Unfortunately most of the obvious history is male. We have to work to find the female part.

A quarter century ago, when women's history first became a popular topic, its study was largely limited to that of the well-known suffragists and their struggle to gain the vote. Now the horizon has expanded considerably. It is realized that anywhere there is history, there is women's history. The trick is not to overshadow one with the other, but to keep it all in perspective.

When Captain Philip Minch, the owner of the Minch shipping interests, died in 1867, control of the company fell to his wife, Anna C. Minch. When the Minch and Steinbrenner families united in 1901, she became president of the new Kinsman Transit Company. The *Anna C. Minch*, her namesake vessel, was lost with all hands on November 11, 1940, near Pentwater, Michigan, on Lake Michigan.

The Anna C. Minch, *lost on Lake Michigan with all hands on November 11, 1940. Lake Superior Maritime Museum.*

Work in offices and telephone exchanges began to open for women.

The last part of the nineteenth century saw the breaking down of many barriers for women. It was discovered that advanced education did not damage their health as once believed. Wealthy girls went to college. The daughters of working class began to find employment as schoolteachers and in factories. They worked in business offices, ran telephones and telegraphs. The right to vote continued to be fought over and won state-by-state.

While women living in the Great Lakes area were aware of their progress, those who worked the water were still stuck in the same old jobs. Rich women may have followed their husbands into yachting and become very competent sailors, but saltwater or fresh, few women advanced from stewardess or cook to the quarterdeck, and then only under extraordinary circumstances.

This book is an attempt to bring at least some of their many stories to the forefront. It is not a disciplined examination of their historical contributions. It does not weigh those contributions or seek to assign a value. There were women divers, salvagers, vessel captains and lighthouse keepers. The female cooks were important

Many people believed a woman belonged at home. Stonehouse Collection.

members of the old schooner crews. It should be remembered that although the contributions of these women may be fewer than men, they are by no means less meaningful. For example, Goodman was an early Great Lakes salvager. She was however, a rarity, perhaps the only female salvor. When a history of Great Lakes salvagers is written, the great preponderance will be men. This does not diminish her role, but it does place it in perspective.

One of the problems encountered was the lack of primary material. The diaries or letters of captain's wives that may have sailed with their husbands during the height of Great Lakes sail are few. In contrast, there is a great deal of material for their saltwater sisters who sailed the world in their husbands great booming square-riggers in voyages lasting years.

I can only conclude that the oceangoing ladies had the luxury of time, while those on the lakes, faced with much shorter trips, did not. The result for future generations is a good record of female seagoing experience and a poor one for the lakes.

Throughout world maritime history, women have served secretly as sailors. Only a very few served openly. Others, more typically, disguised as men, they endured the foul forecastles and 'tween-decks without complaint. Women helped "man" the guns in the British fleet at Trafalgar when Nelson smashed the French. Some served as pirates in the Caribbean Sea. Official histories usually have little mention of these seagoing women. Many were eventually discovered, perhaps when injured and brought to the surgeon or captain for attention, or after death when the sailmaker traditionally sewed the corpse into the canvas bag for the final drop to Davy Jones' Locker.

Determining the numbers of females who sailed disguised as males, on saltwater and freshwater is of course impossible. But we know at least some did it. Their cases are often ethereal, floating on the wind, a short paragraph in a newspaper or logbook noting the discovery of such a situation, or the details of a waterfront rumor. For example, Marine Historian Steve Harold of the Manistee County Historical Society in Manistee, Michigan, remembered finding a short news article telling of an incident on Lake Michigan. A sailor had fallen from a freighter, then grabbed a trailing line. His yells for help went unanswered and apparently he was never missed by his shipmates. Finally after about four hours someone heard his feeble cry and he was hauled back aboard. First aid for the frozen sailor did no good and he soon died. While performing the first aid, the crew discovered that the "he" was a "she."[1]

There are several challenges to doing this kind of book. There is a tendency for example to imply equality for a women doing the same job as a man. It some instances this was true. For example, there likely is no difference between a woman cook and a male cook on a vessel. The tasks done by each were identical. In the case of lighthouse keepers, there was a difference. Female keepers did not paint the tower, that was a job contracted out or given to a male assistant keeper. Nor did they do other "heavy" work around the station.

Whether this distinction was made because of the women being perceived as the "weaker" sex thus reflecting the times, or through a genuine inability of the keepers to do such work, is moot. The point is that the female keepers did not do all of the routine tasks of their male counterparts, thus they can not be fairly compared.

Even today, female soldiers in the Army holding the same MOS (Military Occupational Skill) as a man will often, by subtle social interactions, not perform all the same jobs as the male. In practice, the female will tend not to do the heavy tasks with the men picking up the slack. While this is all in obvious contradiction of official policy, it is still the way of the world.

When all is said and done, however, the women in this book are truly remarkable and should certainly be inspirations for all of us.

CHAPTER ONE

INTO THE DEEP

MARGARET CAMPBELL GOODMAN

Back in the 1920s and 1930s, there was a female marine salvager on the Great Lakes–Margaret Campbell Goodman. She seems not to have been a working salvager in the mold of a Kidd or Reid, taking on all jobs, big or small, as they came. Goodman appears to have focused on the "treasure" wrecks, those with high value cargo, rather than do the mundane work of hauling ships off reefs and shoals, lightering cargo and the other realities of the workaday world of salvage. A petite woman said to weigh less than 100 pounds, and 4 feet, 11 inches in height, her background was in advertising. She was, judging from newspaper stories of the period, an excellent self-promoter. Hailing originally from Brooklyn, New York, she spent much of her time living in Detroit. In various news stories she claimed to be the only woman "deep-sea" diver in the country!

Her first known salvage effort was on the 200-foot wooden passenger propeller *Pewabic*. The vessel was downbound on Lake Huron when it collided with the upbound propeller *Meteor* in clear weather on August 9, 1865. The accident occurred about seven miles off Alpena, Michigan. Within minutes the *Pewabic* dove for the bottom, taking 75 to 100 people with her, and a rich cargo of 267 tons of copper and iron ore. Some of the copper was in the form of "mass" copper, or pure chunks weighing hundreds or even thousands of pounds. The rest was in ingot form.

Margaret Campbell Goodman during her Pewabic days.

Earlier attempts to salvage the copper were generally unsuccessful. Late in the 1865 season, the owners sent Billy Pike, a famous diver, to start salvage on the *Pewabic*. He was drowned without recovering any valuables. Between 1880-1884, two or three more divers were killed on the wreck. In a 1892 effort, diver Oliver Pelkie was killed when his lines fouled the wreck and cut a hole into the rubber of the suit, allowing water to enter. The same crew returned the following year but was unable to locate the wreck. In 1898, the American Wrecking Company from Milwaukee used a diving bell in an effort to salvage the copper. The bell was a hexagonal-shaped cage made of boiler iron. Once the *Pewabic* was located, diver George Campbell and deckhand Pedar Olsen descended in the bell, but fouled the wreck. After 12 hours of struggle the bell was finally freed and hauled to the surface but the men were dead as the result of a broken viewing port which allowed water to flood into it.

In 1917, Goodman organized several rich investors and formed a syndicate to salvage the copper from the *Pewabic*. B. F. Leavitt, the inventor of the Leavitt Armored Diving Suit, would provide the mechanism to successfully reach the wreck and then direct recovery operations. The previous October 22, he used the suit to descend to 180 feet in Lake Michigan's Grand Traverse Bay, proving it could withstand the great pressures at the wreck's depths. He later claimed to have made a second Lake Michigan dive to 360 feet.

Leavitt joined the expedition with the goal of making his suit famous and promoting its use on more valuable wrecks. The manganese-bronze armored suit was an effective and useful piece of technology. The arms and legs were made of flexible copper shielded with heavy rubber. Steel fingers which could manipulated by the hands, projected from the arms. An air bottle at the rear provided approximately four hours of

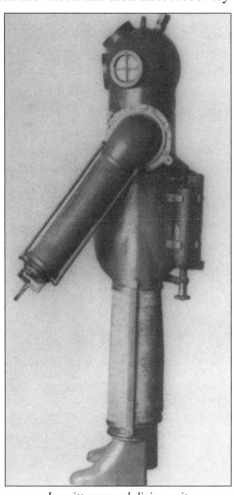

Leavitt armored diving suit.

9

air, regardless of depth. A heavy steel cable lowered the suit into the water and retrieved it. Communications were via a telephone cable.

Goodman chartered the tug *Constitution*, and by May 1917, had located the wreck. The diver reported her on an even keel, with the deck house intact. To prove the identity, he filled a bucket with material and other souvenirs and sent it to the surface. Additional recoveries included a revolver, coins, jewelry, keys and a daguerreotype photo.

Once they were certain of the wreck, Goodman and her crew brought the derrick scow *Eleanor* and went to work with their big clam bucket. Salvage was not a delicate job. With each drop the steel jaws of the bucket dug deep into the *Pewabic*. The diver on the wreck directed the bucket's work. Hauled to the surface, it was centered over the barge and the tag line jerked it open, spilling the contents onto the deck. Wooden cabin pieces, smashed furnishing, miscellaneous items, and somewhere in the dripping mess, a piece of copper or two. Sometimes the amount of copper was substantial. One piece weighed 9,678 pounds. The entire salvage was a tedious process. By July, the amount of copper recovered slowed down considerably. The Leavitt suit was proving not to be as useful as originally thought. The clam bucket stirred up the mud, limiting visibility from its small viewport. Supposedly the salvors recovered

Propeller Pewabic, lost in Lake Huron on August 9, 1865. Stonehouse Collection.

the safe which contained $55,000 in Civil War-era currency. Since the safe had been extensively water damaged, much of the money was not redeemable.

True to her advertising background, Goodman brought up new investors every weekend. Entertainment was provided and the strong push applied to by stock. It all must have been very similar to today's time share sales scams! Leavitt would always make a dive in the suit and describe the wreck on the telephone. Goodman would also make a shallow-water dive. The show was very effective and usually resulted in additional money from the investors. But money did run out. On August 28, the tug company had the sheriff attach the recovered copper, about 70 tons worth, in payment of debts. An additional 50 tons of iron ore were also recovered. A Detroit newspaper would later claim in an article about the ever-newsworthy Goodman, that she recovered $300,000 in copper from the wreck. For this to be true, copper would have had to been valued at $2.00 a pound. The true market value of the copper appears to have been closer to 30 cents per pound.

While the salvage generated a lot of publicity, especially for the diving suit, financially it was a disaster, with the stockholders taking what today would be called a "bath." Goodman and Leavitt apparently never worked together again. Perhaps it was because some newspaper articles claimed she had "personally designed the diving suit and that she directed all the work, going from deck to deck." Leavitt may have taken offense at Goodman receiving the credit for what he had done.

Leavitt later proved to be somewhat of a shady character. Whether Goodman suspected this side of her partner during the *Pewabic* salvage is unknown. For example, his Lake Michigan record dive, in the time he stated, was plainly impossible. Divers knew that if he actually did it, he would have surfaced badly affected by the "bends." Leavitt plainly used the *Pewabic* salvage as a stepping-stone to bigger and deeper things. By 1922 he had raised an estimated $95,000 in shares to salvage a mythical $5 million in gold from the strong room of the steamer *Lusitania*. The

British steamer was sunk by a German submarine off Ireland on May 7, 1915 during World War I, with 1,200 people drowned, including 128 Americans. He promised returns of twenty-to-one, and further recovery from another dozen wrecks he knew of with $127 million in gold and treasure. He dropped out of sight with the money without ever leaving for the *Lusitania*.

Goodman's Great Lakes adventures were not over. A story in the *Cleveland Plain Dealer* of October 30, 1922, announced she was going to start the salvage of the cargo of the schooner *New Brunswick*. Under the command of Captain McTavish, the 138-foot schooner was downbound on Lake Erie when she sank in a gale off Point Pelee on August 26, 1858. The survivors claimed the wind blew 70 miles per hour and the cargo began to shift. There is conflicting evidence on the number of survivors. One source claims five of nine of those aboard were lost, another, that all of the crew made it ashore but the Negro cook. He died in the yawl on the way to the beach.

The masts of the *New Brunswick* stayed above water for at least a year, thus the location of the wreck was locally well known. The water was said to be only 35-40 feet deep. There was no immediate effort to salvage her.

The cargo was said to be black walnut and oak timbers. The paper announcing Goodman's salvage estimated the value at $200,000. Other sources would later claim it to be $500,000. Perhaps her reputation with investors from the *Pewabic* was the problem, but apparently she never went to the wreck at this time.

In an October 11, 1934, article in the *Detroit News*, Goodman announced she was again going for the *New Brunswick's* "wooden treasure." "I am more than 60 years old now and I wouldn't do any of the recovery work myself but will go underwater at least once to look over the site."

Goodman's first job was to find the wreck, a small detail that "wrecked" many a "wreck" salvage. Goodman's plans included using an airplane as a spotting aid. "From a high altitude we should be able to see the wreck. If we can't see it with our eyes maybe the camera plates will catch it. If we have good luck we should locate the wreck and have the cargo on our barge within two weeks. The weather may turn bad on us, however." The news story said the salvage was being backed by a syndicate of Toronto businessmen.

Two years later the *Detroit News* of May 5, 1938, described Goodman's efforts to reach the "fortune in oak and walnut" and claimed the cargo was worth $250,000. It further claimed she had found the wreck in 1934 but foul weather prevented salvage. Why there was a four-year hiatus in activity was not explained. By now Goodman was a woman of 65 years of age and her promoting days were ending. It is likely this was her last hurrah.

The value of the cargo appears to always be wildly exaggerated. In 1938, C. H. P. Snider, a Toronto newspaper marine reporter, "ran the numbers" on the true value of the cargo. Checking with local lumber yards, he priced one- and two-inch walnut at $154-$165 per thousand board feet, and white oak at $98-$118. If the cargo was 115,000 board feet, as usually quoted, the value of it–assuming all was black walnut–was $18,075; if it were all white oak, $13,570. While black walnut improves with submersion, it is doubtful it would have reached a multiple of nearly fourteen times value (on the basis of $250,000).

Who actually discovered the *New Brunswick* is open to question. Goodman claims to have found it in 1934, but this is questionable at best. In August 1938, an expedition organized by "Hickory Joe" Ley and Dexter Goodison gave up their effort. Their diver reported the wreck was smashed up and cargo scattered over the bottom, saying "it was not worth the money." The vessel was on its side, deep in the sand and the other side smashed. He said he only saw one log and it was leaning against the wreck.

The wreck is believed to have been found using side-scan sonar in the mid-1980s and extensively salvaged. However, there was no black walnut aboard, only white oak. The salvor used a crane to recover the logs, which effectively tore the wreck apart. He was unable to sell the wood at a price level sufficient to support his expenses and filed for bankruptcy. When all was said and done, the *New Brunswick* got the last laugh![2]

FRANCIS BAKER, GIRL DIVER

Although Margaret Goodman claimed to be the only female deep-sea diver, a woman a generation before, Francis Baker, was known as the "girl diver of the Great Lakes." Her exploits were recorded by J. Oliver Curwood, a famous writer of adventure novels. His article on Baker was published in the *Woman's Home Companion* magazine in 1905.

Curwood described her as pretty, well-educated and, only 20 years old, stating she was one of the "most fearless and resourceful divers along the Great Lakes." Further, he said, that she had made nearly $25,000 in the last three years in her chosen occupation.

He also gave her credit for the discovery of the wreck of the propeller *W. H. Stevens* and subsequent recovery of $50,000 in copper. Her share was claimed to be a hefty $5,000. The *Stevens*, a wooden package freighter, was lost on September 8, 1902, when she burned and sank in 80 feet of water off Clear Creek, Ontario, west of Long Point on Lake Erie.

Baker's father, Captain H. W. Baker, was a Detroit wrecking captain and she grew up in the business. Many times she watched her father steam away to rescue a ship on the rocks or salvage a cargo. She always wanted to climb aboard the tug and go with him. When she was finally old enough, he relented and she sailed with him sharing his escapades. She used her time with him well, watching and learning the ins and outs of the wrecking business. The intricacies of steam pumps held no mystery for her, or the laying of heavy ground tackle for pulling ships off a rock reef. She mastered the use of wrecking jacks and both concrete and canvas patches. But it was diving that held her attention.

Curwood's article stated her first dive was on a wreck in Lake Huron in 50 feet of water. One of the wreck's owners had lamented the loss of a diamond ring he left in the cabin. Baker volunteered to get it for him. Baker climbed into the heavy canvas diving dress, with 20-pound lead boots and a ponderous brass helmet. Slowly she was lowered over the side and together with one of the experienced men, they made their way to the wreck. Carefully, walking in the cumbersome suit for the first time, she reached the cabin, carefully entered and recovered the ring. When she surfaced and presented it to him, he was so thrilled with her effort on his behalf, he presented it to her as a gift.

Divers at this time earned $50-$200 a day, which meant Baker could earn a considerable income as a working diver. She realized, however, that she was better as a manager of the salvage crew rather than as a simple diver.

Baker had her share of adventures. Finding a body on a wreck was one of them. Her father's company was salvaging a vessel in Lake Huron that had sunk with the loss of only one sailor. He never came ashore. The first salvage divers on the wreck looked for the missing man without success. When Baker dove the wreck, she accidentally came across him, reaching out to her with chalky white arms as if to grab her. She didn't panic, but kept her head and gave the pull on her line, signaling to be hauled to the surface.

In another instance, she was diving a wreck when her air hose disconnected from the pump at the surface. It was reconnected just in time. She once spent 20 minutes entangled in wreckage 50 feet down. Finally she was able to free her rope and signal for help.

Baker's greatest achievement was the salvage of the copper from the *W.H. Stevens*. In the story, she was given full credit for planning the search for the vessel. It took several days of dragging but they found the wreck exactly where she marked it on the chart. She was also the first diver down on it to confirm its identity. Although it took 10 long days to haul the copper up, Baker and the men didn't care. They had found their treasure ship![3]

CHAPTER TWO

COURAGE IN THE FACE OF DANGER

MAEBELLE MASON

We expect grown men to be heroes, to face death straight in the eye, and make courageous rescues. In the 1880s during the height of the Victorian Era, for a young woman to be a "man of action" definitely went against the norm. But Maebelle L. Mason was not an average young woman!

Maebelle was the only child of Orlo J. Mason and his wife, Belle. Born in New York State, he did a variety of jobs until joining a New York volunteer infantry regiment just prior to the outbreak of the Civil War in 1861. Proving a gallant soldier, he fought in many well-known campaigns, and at the wars' conclusion he was discharged with the rank of captain. He used the title for the rest of his life.

In the spring of 1866 he went to Detroit and found work with the Detroit Dry Dock Company as a carpenter. Later he worked for a succession of rail car manufacturers. He also found time for romance, marrying Miss Belle M. Mills, the daughter of a well-known Detroit vessel and tug owner. In 1868, he moved to St. Louis, continuing to work in the rail car trade. Maebelle was born while the couple was in St. Louis. Returning to Detroit in 1882, he found employment again with the famous Pullman Palace Car Company, a firm he had worked for during his original Detroit stay.

In June of 1885, he accepted an appointment as the keeper of the Mamajuda Lighthouse in the Detroit River. Built in 1849, the light marked the dangerous shoal near Grosse Isle. Mason loyally kept the light for nine long years without once having a complaint lodged against him. Considering the tremendous amount of traffic on the river, it was a remarkable achievement.

This, then, was the sort of father he was to his daughter. Maebelle looked up to him. She saw a man whose bravery was demonstrated by his war service, knew hard work from his following the rail car trade, and showed faithfulness from keeping his light in good order–always.

Maebelle was certainly the apple of her father's eye. Bright and energetic, she was very proficient in music as was her mother. As the daughter of a lightkeeper she also learned the craft of handling

Manajuda Light. US Coast Guard.

boats and the intricacies of operating the various complicated lamps and mechanisms. Lightkeeping was always a family affair and she pulled her weight. Living on an island meant using a small boat to reach town and that often meant a long row. Acquiring such skill was second nature to a lightkeeper's daughter!

She was barely 14 years old when she performed an act of courage that attracted the attention of lake mariners everywhere. On May 11, 1890, a man in a rowboat threw a line to the steamer *C.W. Elphicke*, passing down the Detroit River between Mamajuda Lighthouse and Grassy Isle. In the process, he capsized the boat, spilling himself into the swiftly rushing water. Catching a ride with steamers was common on the river, sometimes with dire consequences. Captain Montague of the *Elphicke* was unable to help the man, who was hanging on to his overturned boat and in danger of drowning. When the steamer passed the Mamajuda Lighthouse, Montague signaled there was a man overboard and asked for help.

Captain Mason was gone with the government boat, leaving Maebelle and her mother alone at the light. Whatever action to be taken was up to them. The only boat left was a small, flat bottomed-punt. Heaving together, the pair dragged it to the water and launched it. Of the two women, Maebelle was the better rower, so she took the heavy oars and the two made for the drowning man. After a mile of hard rowing, they reached him. Pulling together, Maebelle and her mother hoisted the exhausted man aboard the punt. Then Maebelle tied the line to the capsized boat to the punt and rowed the long way back to the lighthouse.

When Captain Charles V. Gridley of the US Navy, the inspector of the Tenth Lighthouse District, learned of Maebelle's heroic feat, he recommended her for a lifesaving medal. Gridley was a hero in his own right, having commanded the cruiser *Olympia* at the battle of Manila Bay two years before. His term expired before the award was approved.

The presentation of the silver or second class lifesaving medal was formally made by his successor, Commander E.W. Woodward, at Detroit's Cadillac Hotel during the convention of the Grand

Army of the Republic. Maebelle enchanted the grizzled old veterans. They reported she received the award "...with the naive modesty so charming in a young maiden, believing she had but performed an act of humanity."

Not to be outdone by the government, the shipmasters association presented her with a gold lifesaving medal with a Maltese cross and gold chain attached. It was inscribed:

"Presented to Miss Maebelle L. Mason
for Heroism in saving life

May 11, 1890, by the E.M.B.A.
of Cleveland.

From that day until she was married in June 1892 and left the lighthouse, association vessels saluted the brave girl with their steam whistles when they passed the light.[4]

GULL ISLAND TRAGEDY

Being a hero isn't always about doing something daring, saving lives or risking your own to accomplish a necessary task. Sometimes it's just about carrying on, doing your duty in the most trying of personal tragedy. After all, while you may have suffered irreparable loss, there were still others whose lives depended on your careful and deliberate actions, just as always. A case in point in that of the "Heroine of Gull Rock."

Gull Rock and its associated reefs were especially dangerous and hazardous to vessels running the deep water course between Manitou Island and Keweenaw Point in Lake Superior. Gull Rock itself was about four miles directly off the tip of the Keweenaw. To mark the island, Congress appropriated $15,000 in 1866 to construct a lighthouse. On November 1 of the following year, the light was first exhibited using a fourth order Fresnel lens.

The 46-foot-square brick light tower is attached to a two-story brick keeper's house. Gull Rock stands barely 15 feet above the lake, and perhaps is less than four lighthouses in size. During storms, waves washed completely over the rock and smashed into the house. Although only four miles offshore, it was as lonely a place as could be imagined.

In 1896, the family on the rock consisted of the lightkeeper, his wife, who was also the assistant keeper, their two children, and the keeper's 16-year-old nephew. The oldest child was four and the youngest, two. By all counts, it was a happy little group until the youngest child was struck down with an unknown illness. The worried father decided to go to Copper Harbor, 12 miles to the west on the Keweenaw, where he could get a small tug, then return for the mother and sick child and get them to medical aid. His rowboat was too small to take them with him on the trip to Copper Harbor, especially considering the rolling gale on the lake. In addition, since his wife was the assistant keeper, she would have to remain to keep the light in his absence. Before he could ready the boat for the trip, the child died.

As soon as the gale abated the next day, the keeper rowed to Keweenaw Point and pulled the rowboat ashore. Then he hiked over eight miles to Copper Harbor where he told his sad tale to his friend, the Copper Harbor lightkeeper. As there was no undertaker closer than 40 miles, the keeper made the small coffin for his son with his own hands. Since by now it was dark, he spent the night at the light. The following morning the tug took the keeper, the Copper Harbor keeper, and some friends to Gull Rock, arriving in the early afternoon.

All the while the husband was gone, it was the wife who had to carry on–as a mother to her children, dead and alive, and as an assistant keeper to the tireless demands of the tower beacon. There were no friends to help her mourn or pastor to ease the pain with gospel verses. She was utterly alone with her grief. Silently and sadly she prepared her baby for burial, making a pretty white dress, washing the tiny body and in all ways readying it for the grave. All the while the four-year-old tugged at her apron, demanding a measure of her attention.

All night she sat alone with her lifeless child, keeping both a death vigil and a light watch. When her husband arrived with the tug, she gently kissed her child for the last time and placed him to rest in the coffin, saying in choking voice, "Baby, baby dear, and must we give you up."

There was no place on the rock to hold a burial service, not even a bucket of earth to dig in. There was no pastor to perform the last rites of the church. Solemnly, the small family left on the tug for the mainland. One of the friends remained at the light to keep the watch. This unknown woman, a mother and an assistant light-keeper, was truly a hero twice.[5]

MORGAN OF THE LIFE SAVERS

If a lighthouse keeper's daughter could show heroism, certainly a lifesaving station keeper's daughter could do no less. Edith Morgan, the young daughter of Captain Sanford W. Morgan, the keeper of the Grand Point au Sable Lifesaving Station on the Michigan shore of Lake Michigan, demonstrated her valor twice.

On Saturday, March 23, 1878, a strong north gale rolled across Lake Michigan. The air was bitterly cold and driven hard by the piercing wind, seemed even colder. A man walking on shore spotted two men clinging desperately to the bottom of an overturned boat,

While men launch a surfboat, a woman stays on the beach. Stonehouse Collection.

two or three miles out in the wild lake. The observer ran to the new U.S. Life Saving Service station and notified the keeper. The navigation season hadn't opened yet so Morgan had none of his crew at the station. The keeper was alone, save for his two sons, one of whom was very young, and his daughter Edith. By no stretch could he use his big surfboat with such a small crew. At least four men were needed to handle it in a storm. But there was a small fish boat available and perhaps they could just manage to use it. Morgan assigned his young son the job of steering while he, his older son James, and Edith rowed. Young Edith had grown up with boats and the lake. She took her place on the thwart willingly. She rowed as hard as she could, sending her oar biting deep into the lake with each stroke. But it wasn't to be. Although they managed to fight through the first breakers, by the time they reached the outer bar the boat was nearly swamped and they had to return to shore. Unlike the Life Saving Service's surfboat, it was not self-bailing.

Safe on land, Morgan sent James to town to get a volunteer crew for the surfboat. To avoid delay, Edith and her father cleared a path for the surfboat through the great pile of logs and driftwood that littered the beach. By the time James returned with the volunteers, the work was finished. Edith then helped launch the surfboat and the crew successfully rescued the two men. She certainly would have willingly again taken her seat in the boat had the crew been short a man. In the fish boat she had proven both her strength and courage. When the rescue boats went out, she wanted to go with them!

On December 21 the following year, Edith distinguished herself again during the wreck of the steamer *City Of Toledo*. Again the accident happened after the close of navigation, when the regular life saving station crew had been discharged for the winter.

During the night the steamer had grounded in a thick snowstorm about 300 yards offshore and six miles south of the station. She had been en route from Milwaukee to Ludington, Michigan, with 24 people when she struck. Dawn found her fast in 10 feet of water and broadside to the beach with the cold waves breaking over her. The temperature was far below freezing and she was soon covered with ice. The people on the beach thought she looked more like an iceberg than a ship! Joshua Brown, the lifesaving station

United States Life Saving Service crew launching a surfboat. Stonehouse Collection.

keeper at Ludington, 13 miles south of Grand Point au Sable, first heard of the wreck and took off to find her, arriving at the beach opposite the steamer at 3:00 p.m. He discovered the captain and some of the crew had already come ashore safely, but their lifeboat stove in her side against the ice banks and was unusable. The captain told him a tug had earlier managed to get a line on the steamer. However, a powerful west squall drove her off. The men left on the ice-covered steamer were now in great danger, both from freezing and the ship breaking up under them. Keeper Brown started north in an attempt to get help from Sanford Morgan at Grand Point au Sable. On the way he met Morgan and Edith coming south with the surfboat and a six-man volunteer crew. Keeper Morgan had also learned of the wreck. The keeper and his men launched the surfboat at nearby Hamblin Harbor and pulled for the wreck. Whether Edith stayed ashore or accompanied the men is unknown. It's hard to believe she would have willingly stayed safe on the beach as the men went out to face danger. She wasn't the kind of girl to avoid action!

The combination of rough water, cold weather and an untrained crew defeated the volunteers. Effectively using the surfboat in rough water is a skill learned only after long hours of drill. The men were willing, but their inexperience defeated them. As soon as they made it past the harbor piers the boat swamped in the breakers. Thick ice clogged the thole-pins, the wooden pegs that held the oars in place, and covered the oars, making them nearly useless, and they were forced to return.

The beach cart was then brought up and after carefully sighting in, Morgan fired the Lyle gun and neatly dropped the shot line across the wreck on the first try. The sailors on the wreck cautiously hauled the thin line aboard, then the heavier whip line. Following the directives on the placard, the sailors made the hawser fast to the highest point on the ship they could reach, in this case the hurricane deck. Ashore, the men followed Morgan's directions for rigging the sand anchor, raising the scissors and hauling out the big hawser. Untrained in the complicated maneuvers, it took longer than usual

United States Life Saving Service practicing the breeches buoy drill. Stonehouse Collection.

to finish the job. Finally, they attached the breeches buoy to the suspended line and hauled it out to the wreck. Edith, who had watched her father drill his crew in the highly choreographed operation many times, was a great help in showing the men how the gear had to be rigged.

Since the hawser could be mounted no higher than the hurricane deck, the line "bellied" into the water. As the sailors were pulled ashore, more than half of the distance they were dragged through the freezing surf. The current was running fast, at an estimated five miles per hour, putting a tremendous strain on the rigging and adding greatly to the effort of the men pulling the lines ashore. Edith took her place alongside the men, and for five long hours she lent her strength to the struggle as well as encouraged the others to keep at it.

Short-handed and perched precariously on an ice bank, the shore crew had a exhausting battle. Standing 15 inches deep in wet snow made the work more arduous. Snow and stinging hail struck constantly. The whip line became stiff with ice further compounding the fight to get the crewmen ashore. Plainly, the breeches buoy could not continue to be used under such conditions.

Morgan decided to go back to the surfboat. First he looped the painter over the whip line. Then, with three volunteers, he shoved it into the water and together they hauled themselves hand-over-hand through the surf and out to the wreck. Once alongside they took aboard a dozen of the crew and returned to the shore the same way. The high ice banks prevented them from running the boat up on the beach as was usual, so Morgan had the men leap into the water and some of the crowd that had by now gathered to watch the drama, helped them to safety. Edith was again in the thick of things, waist deep in the icy surf, pulling the men to safety. Morgan and his volunteers went out to the wreck for a second trip and rescued the remainder of the crew, including one woman. As a last action, Morgan used the crowd to assist in hauling the heavy surfboat over the ice banks to shore. It would be needed again and losing it was not the way of the old Life Saving Service.

In recognition of the great contributions Edith made on both rescues, she was awarded a silver lifesaving medal. It was testified that without her assistance, some of those aboard the steamer would surely have perished.[6]

The Silver Life Saving Medal was the second highest award for lifesaving. Stonehouse Collection.

FALLING TOWER

The single idea burned into the soul of every lightkeeper was the importance of protecting the lamps and lenses from damage of any kind. On the Bois Blanc Island in northern Lake Huron, just to the east of the Straits of Mackinac, it was the keeper's sister who was left to carry through when disaster struck. Bois Blanc Light was built in 1829, making it the second oldest light on the lake. Construction of these early lights was often of poor quality.

In January 1838, a terrific gale struck the area. Eber Ward, the lightkeeper from 1829-42, had gone over to Mackinac Island and the sudden storm prevented his return. Left on the island was his sister, Emily, and her adopted child. Alone they had to face the appalling onslaught of wind and wave.

The stone tower had been built too close to the water, and years of erosion had resulted in the it becoming dangerously close to the lake. The house was separate from the tower but close enough that, should the tower fall, it could land on it.

As the storm increased in ferocity, waves washed around the base of the tower and smashed into it, shaking the structure. Thanks to Emily, the light still burned bright, sending a true beam out to sailors on the wild lake. Finally Emily realized the obvious, that the tower would soon go over! It was up to her to save the precious lamps and lenses! Eber had always stressed the importance of the equipment and she could not let him down.

She left the child watching out the window of the house as she dashed into the tower. As quickly as she could, she climbed the 150 steps to the lamproom. She took a minute to stand and gaze in wonder at the wild scene before her, the powerful waves striking the rocky shore sending tremendous sheets of spray skyward. Great black clouds scudded by overhead. Then she went to work disassembling the lenses and lamps and struggling with them to the ground. It took her five trips to bring all the equipment down to safety.

Her work done, she returned to the house and ate dinner. Then she and her child sat at the window watching the tower for the first sign of collapse. In the intermittent lightning flashes, she saw a zigzag crack run up the tower. Grabbing her child, the pair fled into the nearby woods. Within minutes, the tower crashed to the ground, but did not hit the house.

Emily, ever the lightkeepers loyal sister, had done the best she could in the absence of her brother. Alone in the midst of the terrible storm, she had saved life and limb as well as the precious and delicate equipment. A new tower was built in 1838. It was replaced in 1868 with the present lighthouse.

ABIGAIL BECKER OF LONG POINT

When ships got into trouble and wrecked in the vicinity of lighthouses, the light keepers often helped rescue the survivors. Sometimes, however, others stepped into the breech. Abigail Becker is a case in point.

Lake Erie's Long Point, located off Ontario's northeast shore, was a dreaded ship trap of terrible renown. The low sand point reaches out to the southeast for 20 deadly miles. Some sources estimated at least 160 vessels met their untimely end either on the point or just off shore. Lucky sailors survived their wrecked vessels. The unlucky ones didn't, and their bones lay buried in the shifting sands. That the crew of the schooner *Conductor* is part of the former category and not the latter is directly due to the heroic efforts of a young Canadian woman, Abigail Becker.

It was November 23, 1854, and the small schooner *Conductor* was heading for Toronto with a full cargo of 8,000 bushels of corn. A strong southwest wind drove her hard but fair and, if all went well, she would soon be safe in port. Henry Beckett was her master and six other men were aboard with him that fateful day.[7] About midnight, a terrific gust carried away the main topsail and without its steady pull, the schooner was soon blown out of control, quickly broaching and falling off into the deep wave trough. Seas crashed aboard the ship with deadly effect, sweeping all before them. Both yawl boats were smashed into splinters. To avoid being washed away, the crew lashed themselves to the ship. Thick swirling snow blotted out their world in a swirl of white.

The dying schooner blew on before the gale. At 4:00 a.m. she thumped to ground several hundred yards off shore and just to the west of Long Point. The crew, of course, had no idea where they were, only that they would surely die–either from the piercing cold or drowning–when the *Conductor* broke up beneath them. Hurriedly they struggled up the ratlines and tied themselves to the rigging high above the billows sweeping over the schooner. The blizzard raged on in all its hellish frenzy.

To this point, the tale is a very typical one involving Great Lakes shipwrecks. Sometime the next day, if still alive, they would be discovered by a local citizen and, if very fortunate, they would be rescued by an ad hoc lifesaving effort. More often, they would be discovered as dead, frozen corpses dangling stiffly from the shrouds, just another tragedy of the lakes.

By early afternoon the blizzard had blown itself out enough for the beleaguered crew to see a tall woman and several children struggling along the barren shore. The woman was Abigail Becker, a 23-year-old Amazon who stood fully six feet tall and weighed in at 215 pounds of muscle and courage. She had gone to the beach to get water for breakfast when she saw the wreck. Abigail was the wife of Jeremiah Becker, a local trapper, fisherman and beach-comber. She was also the mother of nine children, three of her own and six step-children of her husband's. Jeremiah had gone to Port Rowan on the mainland the day prior and the storm had kept him from returning. Abigail was left alone with nine children and one shipwreck!

Assessing the situation, having no boat and the certainty of the schooner's imminent destruction on the breakers, she had to make a quick decision. She had considered going to the Long Point Lighthouse, but it was 14 miles away, too far to go for quick help. Making her mind up, Abigail waved wildly at the men in an effort to get them to jump into the water and swim ashore. Numbed by the cold and storm, they failed initially to comprehend her meaning until she waded out waist deep in the churning water and gestured to them to jump!

While she waited for the crew to get up nerve, she gathered wood and started a roaring bonfire on the beach opposite the wreck. As she waited anxiously for the first man to swim for it, her children scoured the beach for more wood to feed the voracious fire.

Captain Hackett came first. Jumping into a cresting wave, he was driven toward the beach. Swimming, grasping and kicking he made his way through the boiling waves. At a point just short of the beach it was plain he wasn't going to make it. Done in by the cold and storm, he was ready to give up and surrender to the inevitability of a cold, wet death when Abigail struggled out into chin-deep water for him. With Herculean strength, she seized him with one massive hand and dragged him toward the shore. A final wave broke over the pair, sending both tumbling toward the beach. When it receded Abigail stood up, still gripping the near lifeless captain and dragged him to the warmth of the crackling fire. There she fed him hot tea and piled warm blankets around his numbed shoulders. Through chattering teeth, the captain said he had searched for Long Point and the light, but couldn't see the friendly beams in the storm.

When the mate saw his captain successfully reach the shore, he summoned his own courage and jumped into the heaving lake, striking hard for the beach. He, too, faltered when he approached the pounding surf. Abigail again headed for the crashing water. Captain Hackett, although still trying to recover from his experience, went with her, believing in his heart that no mere woman could fight through the waves and rescue his mate. Both splashed into the cold gray waves in an effort to reach the faltering man. A huge wave broke over all three, sending them tumbling head over heels. Long seconds later Abigail battled to her feet, marching resolutely up the beach dragging the mate in one arm and the captain in the other!

Four of the crew came ashore the same way. Having watched Abigail haul the captain and mate ashore, they knew they could make it too! After a hard swim through the breaking surf, Abigail dragged each in turn to the beach. Other than the captain, the men rescued were the mate, John Jones, and four seaman–James Cousen, J. McCauley, and two men known only by their last names, Jerome and Chalmers.

Finally, only the cook was left. He was frozen fast to the rigging. Not by ice but by fear. He was afraid to brave the terrible lake, regardless of Abigail's welcoming embrace. All night long Abigail waited patiently on the beach for the reluctant cook. Around midnight the gale eased, and by morning's gray light the wind had swung offshore enough to beat down the boiling waves between beach and wreck. The lull came just in time. The schooner had lost all her masts save one and it was teetering on the brink of going over. The very still form of the cook was still lashed tight in its iced rigging.

The captain and his crew, with the help of Abigail, built a rough raft from the wreckage of the schooner and carefully made their way to the wreck. They found the cook more dead than alive, but alive none-the-less. Beating the ice off, they cut him loose and gingerly put his prostrate form on the raft and returned to shore.

For six days the crew were the guests of Abigail and her children in her humble driftwood shack. The life of a trapper's wife was not an easy one and there was barely enough food for her brood–let alone seven hungry sailors! But she made do until her husband finally was able to make it back from the mainland.

It is likely the world would have known nothing of Abigail's heroic deed had it not been for the schooner's owner, Captain E. P. Dorr of Buffalo. When his schooner failed to arrive he started looking for it. While speaking with the Long Point lightkeepers the men told him of young Abigail's feat. Overcome with curiosity, he went to see her for himself and was utterly taken with the woman. Abigail had so little, yet she unhesitatingly risked all to save men she never knew. Since she and her children were all shoeless, he measured their feet before leaving. Sometime later a large crate arrived filled with shoes and clothing as well as a little bible for Abigail inscribed in gold letters, "To Abigail Becker, Life Saver of Long Point, Lake Erie, November 1854." She also received a commendation from Queen Victoria.

Dorr did not let the matter rest. Abigail and her eldest daughter were later brought to Buffalo. There they were honored at the American Hotel at a extraordinary dinner given by the Seamen's Union. She was presented with a purse of $1,000 in gold and a special medal by the Life-Saving Association of New York. During the winter the Canadian Parliament passed a motion to award her with a 100-acre farm in Norfolk County, Ontario, near Long Point. Using part of her gold, she built a small house on the land and lived there in peace with her second husband until she died in 1905.

By any standard of any time, Abigail Becker was a most remarkable woman. She saw what needed to be done and did it, without any thought of danger to herself or future reward.

There was a rather strange sequel to the *Conductor* rescue. The wife of the keeper of the Long Point Lighthouse told the tale of another vessel, also wrecked on Long Point several years later. She got the story from a Mrs. Isaac Brown, the wife of an old Port Rowan sailing captain. The tale goes that the schooner, with a cargo of barley, was driven ashore in a gale nearly opposite the Becker home. All of the crew were rescued except for the cook, who could not be found. During the fall as much of the grain cargo was salvaged as possible, and the broken hull left on the beach.

Since the wreck was so close to the Becker house, it became a convenient place for the family to draw their water during the winter. They had no well, so in the winter someone either had to hike a considerable distance out on the bay to get past the weeds or do the same on the lakeside to avoid the shallow sandy bottom. The schooner was the solution. A short walk over the ice banks to the wreck and they could draw clear water from her hold, which acted as a well.

One morning one of her daughters was sent for water, then came running back, saying something about a woman in the wreck waving to her! Abigail returned with her daughter to the schooner. Looking down from the deck into the empty cargo hold, she saw a woman floating in the water. The effect must have been surreal: the darkness of the hold, perhaps pierced by a yellow beam of sunlight cutting into the gloom, the body drifting back and forth in the gentle wave wash with the arms gently waving in the motion. It was a macabre dance of welcome! The woman, of course, was the missing cook. Apparently she was drowned in her berth when the vessel wrecked. Subsequently, the waves had torn down the bulkhead between her cabin and the hold, allowing the body to drift out into the light of day.[8]

HEROINES OF THE *COX*

When the big steel steamer *George M. Cox* smashed into Rock Of Ages Reef in western Lake Superior on May 27, 1933, there were many goats and few heroes. One of the latter was the lightkeeper, John Soldenski. His story and the complete story of the wreck is told in my book, *Lighthouse Tales*. There were also two heroines, Adeline Keeling, the ship's staff nurse, and stewardess Beatrice Cote. Before I explain how both achieved fame, it is necessary to understand something of how the vessel wrecked.[9]

The ship was built in 1901 as the *Puritan*. At 233 feet overall length and 40 feet in beam, she was a proud member of the Graham & Morton Transportation Company fleet. After the company determined they had erred and made her too small, in 1908 she was lengthened by 23 feet.

From her launching until 1918, she made regular runs between Chicago, Benton Harbor and St. Joseph and Mackinac Island, carrying excursionists happy to be enjoying their time on the lake. The Michigan Transit Company took over the vessel in 1918, and later the U.S. Navy, which used her as a transport and training

The steamer George M. Cox ready to start a new season. Stonehouse Collection.

vessel during World War I. When the war ended, she returned to the Great Lakes passenger trade. The effects of the Great Depression sent her to lay-up in Manistee, Michigan.

In 1933, George M. Cox, a New Orleans lumber and shipping tycoon, purchased her and the steamer *Isle Royale*. He intended to operate both vessels in a new passenger service between Chicago and Mackinac Island, as well as other Lake Michigan ports and as far north as Thunder Bay on Lake Superior. In addition, the company would run day cruises out of Chicago. Since the Century of Progress Exposition was soon to open in Chicago, Cox foresaw no shortage of passengers.

The Century of Progress Exposition was intended to commemorate the 100th anniversary of the founding of Chicago. It opened on May 27, 1933, coincidently the same day the *Cox* hit Rock of Ages Reef! The exposition, now largely forgotten, was held on Lake Michigan, immediately south of the city's downtown district. The fair site is presently occupied by Meig's Field and McCormick Place. The exposition was popular and ran for two years, a year longer than originally planned. Today it is mostly remembered for the famous exotic and fan dancer, Sally Rand!

The old steamer was completely refurbished inside and out. The owner wanted her to be in tiptop shape for the start of what he was sure would be a very profitable enterprise. On May 24, 1933, the *Cox* left Manistee and when she reached Chicago, was given a brass band welcome. Patricia Kelly, the young daughter of Chicago's mayor, Ed Kelly, rechristened her *George M. Cox*.

During this time, there was a fair amount of "hanky panky" on some of the passenger vessels running out of Chicago. The old "Roaring Twenties" hadn't ended yet! Before taking the vessel from Manistee, George M. Cox told the press, "The boats are elegantly equipped and everything that can possibly be done will be offered for the passengers' pleasure. The ships however, are going to remain clean, there'll be no gambling or disorder if we have to sink them first!"

The *Cox* departed Chicago on her first trip nearly empty of paying passengers with the intention of picking up a load of 250 people in what is now known as Thunder Bay, Ontario (then the twin cities of Fort William and Port Arthur) on Lake Superior. The city officials of Thunder Bay were excited about the steamer coming and a large celebration was planned, complete with brass band and local dignitaries. Aboard for the run were 32 personal guests of the owner and 89 crew, including sailors, engine room gang, cooks, entertainers and stewardesses. The cruise up the lakes was uneventful, locking through the Soo, then stopping at Marquette and Houghton, Michigan on the south shore of Lake Superior.

At about 2:00 p.m., on May 28, 1933, the *Cox* pulled away from the Houghton dock and out into the Keweenaw Waterway. About and hour and a half later she reached the open lake and took a course for Rock of Ages Light at the south tip of Isle Royale. At the light, she would turn for Thunder Bay.

After a while the steamer ran into fog. Later, some of the witnesses said it was just patchy, others that it was like pea soup. Some claimed the *Cox* reduced speed. Others said no change was made and she kept running full ahead. What was not in dispute was that at about 6:25 p.m. the steamer ran hard up on Rock of Ages Reef, hitting the rocks with disastrous force. The *Cox* literally tore her bottom out on the reef.

When the SOS went out, the Coast Guard responded with the 125-foot cutter *Crawford* from Two Harbors, Minnesota, 125 miles to the southwest, and a 36-foot motor lifeboat from Portage, Michigan, 40 miles to the south.

Seeing the masts of the steamer above the low fog and watching them suddenly turn into the reef, lightkeeper Soldenski came out in his power lifeboat to render what help he could. After the confusion at the wreck was sorted out, he towed all of the steamer's passengers and crew in their lifeboats to the light station. It offered very poor shelter but was the best he could do. There was no lighthouse as such with traditional keeper's quarters, just a 130-foot-high stone tower with a concrete landing stage.

The Cox "on the rocks." Lake Superior Marine Museum.

All night long the survivors huddled and shivered at the cold light tower. Since it was too small for everyone to get inside, they had to take turns. They even perched on the spiral staircase. When the Portage lifeboat arrived, it shifted 43 survivors to the Singer Hotel at Washington Island, eight miles away on Isle Royale. At 6:30 a.m., when the *Crawford* arrived, she picked up the survivors from both the tower and hotel and returned them to Houghton.

The freighter *Morris Tremaine* also responded to the call for help. After standing by offshore, Cox, nurse Keeling, stewardess Cote and the two injured men were loaded aboard. The freighter took them to Port Arthur, where the nearest hospital was located.

When the steamer hit the reef, many of the guests had just sat down for supper. Tables and chairs slid across the deck. Fine china and crystal smashed to the deck. Trays of hot food flew into the air, and the stewardesses carrying them were thrown to the deck. The orchestra was thrown into a heap. Steam hissed out in great clouds from broken pipes torn apart by the force of the impact. Everywhere there were cries of the injured.

The passengers and crew milled about in confusion building to panic. The steamer was high on the reef, with an estimated 110 feet of her bow out of the water, and listing nearly 45 degrees to port. First reports claimed 50 people were injured in the crash. Three were hurt seriously, one man with a broken leg, Stewardess Cote with a suspected broken back, and another seriously burned man from a vat of boiling fat, who would die nearly a year later of his injuries.

It was now that heroines emerged from the disaster. One was Adeline Keeling, the ship's 23-year-old staff nurse. After the crash she worked continuously for nearly 24 hours supervising the care of the injured. She was also hurt when she tripped over an oar during the evacuation of the ship. The *Fort William Times-Journal* later commented that it was "her generalship that won the admiration of the rescued and George M. Cox." Interviewed after the wreck, when the *Tremaine* docked at Port Arthur with the three seriously injured crew, she was described as a "mere slip of a girl,

The lonely Rock of Ages Light. US Coast Guard.

barely more than five feet in height, her beautiful long dark curls flowing in the early morning breeze, nurse Keeling, despite her long period of wakefulness, had a smile on her pretty face and her dark eyes were sparkling as she was met by a reporter." The newspaper account continued:

> Although she had been nursing the patients throughout the long trip from the scene of the wreck to port, she was in attendance on Miss Beatrice Cote, 21, schoolgirl chum, and stewardess of the *Cox*, who was suffering from painful injuries to her back and side as the boat docked.
>
> Nurse Keeling was concerned gravely as to the injuries of the patients and despite the fact that the

sisters at the St. Joseph's Hospital, the institution where the patients were removed to by ambulance, asked her to go to bed and rest for a few hours, she declined.

It was not until the x-rays of both Miss Cote and Alexander Mack (the injured crewman) were taken and it was found their injuries were not serious, that Miss Keeling consented to rest for a few hours. Nurse Keeling gave a few minutes of her time to relate her story in the waiting room of the hospital. Her nurse's uniform was all the attire she had saved from the wreck. The white uniform was soiled and spotted with blood from the injured.

"It was simply dreadful and I would not care to experience the same thing for any money" said Nurse Keeling. However, she added she was ready to board the steamer *Isle Royale* and take over her professional duties when the big boat commences its regular service.

"We left Chicago on Wednesday afternoon," related Nurse Keeling. "We had a warm reception when we arrived there that morning. The boat was in first class condition and I was excited as it was my first trip in this capacity. We stopped in Houghton, Hancock and Marquette and received civic receptions in each place. On leaving Houghton the weather was all that a sailor could wish for with the sun shining brightly practically all day long," she said. "About five o'clock we headed into patches of fog which gradually thickened," she continued. "The boat continued at a fast clip, 17 miles an hour I believe it was. The heavy fog enveloped us. It certainly was foggy."

"However, this did not worry us and when we went down to dinner shortly after six o'clock everyone was in a happy frame of mind. I was happy because I had just finished a 12 hour stretch on duty and was glad to sit down and enjoy the evening meal knowing I could turn in shortly after. It was a beautiful dinner with the orchestra playing soft, dreamy waltz numbers. If anyone had told me that such a thing as a shipwreck was going to take place at such a time as this, I would have thought them off their heads. It was undreamed of entirely."

"I heard the fog horn blowing and warning the vessel, but I paid no attention. Without warning there was a sickening, crunching crash, the noise of which was deafening. A second later there was a second, louder crash and I felt the fast moving boat come to a quick stop and turn over on her port side."

"It was a terrible experience. Women began to scream. Everything on the table was thrown to the floor. I was in the act of pouring some water from the water glass and it was spilled all over my dress. Everyone was thrown to the floor and all slid toward the lower side along with tables, chairs and every movable object. A huge buffet that was about fifteen feet in length came shifting at a speedy clip across the floor in our direction. It was the buffet that caught me a glancing blow and knocked me into a stateroom."

"Dazed from the blow, I was unable to assist myself for a few minutes but Beatrice Cote–I believe I owe my life to her, she said–came to my rescue and assisted my to my feet and along with the rest we climbed out to the starboard deck which was high above us. We were forced to pull ourselves up the slanting floor by means of grabbing the poles."

"'As I was climbing out of the dining hall, I looked back and to my horror saw the room from which I had been assisted by a few minutes before, had filled with water. It gives me a creepy feeling to think about it."

"Funny though," she pondered, "How one can take it when probable death is staring you in the face." She then took from her pocket her Catholic Mission cross which she fondled tenderly. "It is strange really, that of all my belongings, this was all that I saved."

Nurse Keeling was reticent about mentioning the fact that she was one of the last to leave but this was learned for other sources. When approached on this, she replied that she was too busy taking care of the injured to think about herself. She, however, stated she saw to it that all the injured were safely stowed in the boats before she left the stranded steamer. "It took very little time for the power launch driven by the lighthouse keeper to pilot the five lifeboats and two rafts to shore," she continued. "It certainly was a pitiful sight to see all those people gathered about and in the lighthouse. Many of the ladies were without their overcoats or hats and were dressed only in light dresses. Many members of the crew were without any clothing as they were in bed when the boat struck and had not had time to get their clothes. The maids lent them their aprons to wrap around themselves," she said.

"Everyone was simply wonderful and the women especially bore up well and when the bandages gave out all hurriedly gave of their lingerie to use as bandages."

"I cannot say too much about the assistance rendered by the woman at the lighthouse. In less than no time she had steaming hot coffee ready for the rescued and the atmosphere became more and more cheery. There was not a drop of liquor on board and the coffee was the only stimulant handy with which to treat the injured."

"I was too busy caring for the three seriously injured members of the crew and I did not take the time to size up the situation to any great extent, but once in a while the fog would lift and it certainly was a painful sight to see the beautiful white ship keeled over on her side and stranded on that hidden reef. The whole front of her was stove in. Deck chairs were floating in the water."

"It was a welcome sight to see the steamer *Tremaine* come and stand-by. We lost no time in placing the injured in the power launch and Mr. Cox and myself accompanied them on the trip. Once on board the freighter we received every possible attention. The captain and crew were at our service at all times and did everything to make the patients as comfortable as could be. Members of the crew gave up their bunks for us, but I could not sleep."

Stewardess Beatrice Cote not only freed her friend Adeline from the flooding stateroom, but also helped many passengers. In her words, "I was jammed by flying pieces of furniture and painfully hurt. Others were sent sprawling head foremost into the pile of tables and chairs at the foot of the inclined floor. A waitress was held as in a vice by a heavy buffet table which slid the width of the boat and crashed against the port wall. Scores suffered painful bruises and cuts to head and body from flying glass and cutlery."

As stewardess of the vessel, Miss Cote assisted the guests to ferret out and don their life preservers. Owing to the extreme list at which the boat lay, it was difficult to obtain entrance to the staterooms on the starboard side of the vessel where many of the life preservers were located. Finally she was overcome by the injury suffered in the crash and collapsed.

"Owing to the injury in my back, I was placed on a mattress in the bottom of one of the lifeboats but when the power launch from the lighthouse came alongside, I was transferred to it. In making the transfer, one of the members of the crew, a large burly man, slowly lowered me into the powerboat but in doing so slipped. I fell on my back on the engine with the man falling on top of me."

"The pain was almost unbearable but finally we reached the lighthouse where I was carried up the spiral staircase to the top of the tower. Later that evening I was transferred with two other injured crew members to the steamer *Tremaine*. The only way they could get me down was to place me on a mattress and slowly slide me down. My back bumped on each step. The descent to water level was a nightmare."

"For more than an hour the lighthouse boat felt its way through the heavy fog blanket until finally the dark form of the freighter loomed through the mist ahead of us. Stretchers were lowered and one by one we were hoisted to the deck. On the way up I almost slipped off the stretcher as it hovered over the lighthouse powerboat. The trip to Port Arthur was uneventful and I feel much better now after the rest I have had at the hospital."

Keeling and Cote were considered heroines of the wreck. The following reminiscences from Bessie Carter, one of the housekeepers, takes a little different view of events. Remember, however, it was written in 1976, 43 years after the wreck.

I was hired as housekeeper while the boat was being readied. Mr. Cox hired most of the workers from Manistee, such as painters, carpenters, machinists. It took quite a while to get it in ship shape.

We made our first trip to Chicago on May 25, 1933 for supplies and also a cook stove. An open house was held with over five hundred visiting the boat with refreshments being served. We arrived back in Manistee the next day late in the afternoon. We all left the boat for a short time to say goodbye to our families. My lady friend walked me to the boat and we said our goodbyes. I told her to send me roses if anything happened. The boat left around 5 o'clock going up to and thru the Soo Locks that night and then on to Marquette, when again we held an open house. Many people took advantage to look the boat over. There were several vases of lilacs and the visitors were very surprised to see these beautiful bouquets as they were just starting to bud there.

Something happened to the food that we had the night before as several of us felt somewhat ill. Captain Johnson, not feeling well, took a nap. Captain Gilbert relieved him for a while. When Captain Johnson returned to duty he noticed that the ship's compass wasn't right. He tried to get back on course. It was foggy and one could not see very far out over the lake and the wind was blowing very hard. It was getting near supper time and one of the dishwashers told me to look out, there was something way off, straight up out of the water. One boy said that he had been on the lake before but had never seen anything like that before. We were all busy with preparation for the evening meal. I was dishing up the dessert. The dining room was filled with the boat's officers and guests including Mr. Cox and wife and the secretary's wife and mother. I was sitting on the ice chest waiting to serve more ice cream to the guests when suddenly the boat hit something. Everything stopped. The bells were ringing as I looked around and saw the boys sliding across the floor. They made it to the upper deck. The dishes by the steam table fell to the floor like leaves from a tree. The coffee urn spilling coffee all over the floor. The fellow who dished food from the steam table left and I was all alone in the galley.

Miss Carter remembered what happened after transfer to the hotel. Most Of the help did not have their supper. "When we got to it, the owner of the lodge had only been there one day, therefore, not too much food was available (coffee and 30 dozen eggs)," she recalled. " She graciously offered what she had. The chef boiled the eggs and made coffee. That was all we had to eat. Around noon a large Coast Guard cutter removed us off the island and the 2nd chief and myself took over the galley."[10]

The official inquiry of the wreck conducted at Houghton, Michigan, by the U. S. Steamboat Inspection Service, produced some real fireworks. In the official report of loss, Captain Johnson of the *Cox* stated he had "reduced to moderate speed and changing course from the northwest to west after the sound of siren at Rock of Ages Light became more distinct." This was the turning action the lightkeeper saw. Evidently the fog had distorted the sound

Voyaging on a deck chair was not an option for most women on the lakes.
Stonehouse Collection.

enough to confuse the captain as to direction. The first mate, who had the watch from leaving the Portage Upper Entry until she hit the rocks, was accused by the captain of not steering the proper course. Although the mate fiercely denied the captain's claim, testimony by other crew backed up the charges.

Later in the inquiry, testimony by witnesses claimed the mate deserted his post immediately after the collision. Some said he was the first man off the ship! Under the strong questioning, the mate broke down and cried, raging that he was "being framed by a bunch of crooks!" Later he came to blows with the vice president of the line.

The ship proved a total loss, although much of the cargo and material was salvaged, both officially and unofficially. The wreck stayed on the rocks for at least a year before the storms shattered her, sending the remains into the cold depths of the lake.[11]

While the *Cox* produced no heroes, it did spawn two heroines, Adeline Keeling and Beatrice Cote, two crew members who did their duty. Today, many people know the story of the wreck, but few are aware of the contributions of these two young women.

FIRE ON THE *OCEAN WAVE*

Just traveling on the lakes could be dangerous, especially during the early days of steam navigation when shipboard fire was an ever present-danger. There were some terrible examples of steamer fires. On August 9, 1841, the steamer *Erie* burned in Lake Erie with the loss of 175 persons. November 21, 1847, saw the loss of the steamer *Phoenix* on Lake Michigan with 247 killed. The death figures are estimates only. Since records were very poor and no one was certain just how many people were even aboard.

What follows are two newspaper accounts of the loss of the steamer *Ocean Wave* on Lake Ontario. As you read through them, think of the desperation the women passengers faced just from their manner of clothing. Whether in unwieldy hoop skirts or long night dresses, moving over the burning decks and into the lifeboats or

The Erie was typical of many tragic steamboat fires. Lake Superior Marine Museum.

onto floating wreckage must have been incredibly difficult. In the case of one of the women, her night clothes actually saved her life as we will see!

Oswego Daily Times, Monday, May 2, 1853

Terrible Calamity on Lake Ontario
Steamer *Ocean Wave* Burnt and 28 Lives Lost

Ogdensburgh, April 30, 9 P.M.–Loss of the Steamer *Ocean Wave*.–About one o'clock on the morning of Saturday, the 30th of April, 1853, a cry of fire was raised. The Captain and passengers were all in bed. Immediately on the cry of fire, all rushed down to the after part of the boat, and a scene of confusion took place which baffles the imagination to conceive–the cry of children, the wailing of mothers, the parting of friends, were heartrending in the extreme. It was impossible to get at the boat, as the fire was first observed on the upper decks, and in

about half an hour the whole of the upper cab of the saloon was consumed.

The passengers threw themselves out on the planks and on such things as they could get their hands on. Some made for shore (we were about two miles from shore,) others remained clinging to the boat, and those that did so were saved, in number four cabin passengers, 14 of the crew, and the Purser. About half-past four we were delivered from our perilous situation by the schooner *Emblem* of Bronte, Capt. Bolger, and the *Georgiana*, of Port Dover, Capt. Henderson, to whose exertions, through Almighty God, we owe our lives, and we would now most cheerfully tender them our most sincere thanks for their timely assistance, and also for their kindness and attention to our several wants; and particularly to Capt. Bolger of the *Emblem,* for the prompt measures he took to return us to Kingston, and we now ask of the Almighty God to protect him and his in like manner, as he has done us.

Since receiving the above, we have obtained from the Purser the following information:

Passengers Saved.

Mrs. Stevenson, of Hamilton; Mrs. French of Cornwall, Capt. and Mrs. Kiah, Ogdensburgh. Of the lost, or those supposed to be lost, the Purser could only recollect the following names: Mrs. McDonald, Ogdensburgh; Miss McLellan, Cornwall; Mrs. Stewart, Toronto; Mrs. Stevenson's three children and nurse; Miss Gironard (lady's maid;) Lyman Richardson (colored man, on his way to this city with apples;) O'Doyle, from the rear of Brockville; the engineer, bartender, steward and cook."

Oswego Daily Times, Friday, May 6, 1853

Wreck of the Ocean Wave
Statement of the Second Mate

Ogdensburgh, May 2, 5-1/2 o'clock, P.M.–By arrival of the steamer *Ottawa*, we are placed in possession of more facts in relation to the burning of the ill-fated steamer *Ocean Wave*. We give the statement of Mr. Potter, second Mate:

It was my watch. James Stead was at the wheel. Had been walking about the hurricane deck for half an hour previous, and noticed the sparks from the chimney falling thickly on the deck. A number of particles arrested my attention having fallen in one spot and remaining lighted for a long time. The fire occurred as near as I remember, about half past 1 or 2 o'clock.

On looking toward the engine, I discovered a light shining on the piston, and which shown like a lamp. I spoked to the wheelsman and called his attention to the light; then ran aft to the engine and looked down through the openings. As I did so, the flames burst out from below. I immediately gave the alarm by blowing the steam whistle, and went below to wake the crew, and then left to get out the small boats. The fire spread with such rapidity that scarcely five minutes elapsed before the boat was completely enveloped in flames.

While I was below, I saw Capt. Wright rushing forward with the ladies with no other dress but their night clothes. Capt. Wright almost immediately returned to the after gangway, where he shoved over a carpenter's bench, and jumping into the water, got on to it. The greatest consternation and confusion prevailed, so that no order was observed, to save the passengers, but myself and several of the crew endeavored to get out the boats, but found them so badly burned as to be of no use.

Seeing them all leaving the steamer, by various means, I sought my own safety, and succeeded in getting upon the rudder post. There were a half dozen or so, already collected there, and among them Mr. Oliver, the purser. Mr. Oliver is not a swimmer, but he seemed regardless of his own fate, in his manifest endeavors for the safety of others.

The engine stopped within five minutes after the first fire broke out. As we were crowded on the rudder post, I thought it best to change my quarters. I accordingly swam around to the waterwheel. After reaching that I found a woman partially insensible, floating in the water. As she floated along towards me, I reached out my hand and got hold of her, and helped her up on to the wheel. She proved to be Mrs. Stevenson, of Hamilton. She was much exhausted. I managed to get her up on the wheel and near the fire, where we remained about an hour, where we succeeded in getting nearly dry.

She seemed to be inspired with new courage, and devised means for her own safety she took my neck-handkerchief and tied it around her waist, to provide other lashing she tore her night cloths into strips. I was fearful that the piller blocks of the wheel would be burnt away, and accordingly got on the brace forward of the wheels, Mrs. Stevenson following. I left Mrs. Stevenson on the brace; the sparks coming down set her clothes on fire. I prevailed on her to drop into the water, to put out the fire. We worked our way forward by the braces; and while doing so, the outside of the wheelhouse fell out, which made quite a raft, which I got on to and succeeded in getting Mrs. Stevenson on.

The mast which had fallen, had the bell attached, and was a short distance from us, and I pulled for, and got on to it, rang the bell. This brought to our assistance a small boat from a schooner, supposed to be the *Georgiana*, who took us on board–This boat made several trips between the schooner and the wreck, taking off all from it. The first time this small boat approached the sufferers, it came very near, and turned away without taking any one on boats. This movement being observed by the cook, who was clinging to the rudder post, the poor fellow in the agony of despair, let go his hold and perished."

Although Mrs. Stevenson survived, her three children and maid were all lost, either by drowning or burning. None of the various newspaper accounts ever included the nurse's name. As part of the Stevenson household, this was not unexpected. She was just relegated to historical oblivion. [11]

SADIE BLACK OF THE *HANNA*

The great storm of 1913 is often considered the worst ever to hit the Great Lakes. Running from November 6-11, it devastated shipping. Approximately 250 sailors were drowned and 17 vessels completely wrecked. Fifteen of them were steel steamers and represented a loss of over $7 million, a staggering sum for the time. Eleven of the ships were lost with all hands!

Many heroes emerged from the terrible storm but perhaps the most unlikely was Sadie Black, the cook on the big steel steamer *Howard M. Hanna Jr.* She was the wife of the steward, Clarence Black. The steamer had left Lorain, Ohio on Friday, November 8, with a full load of coal bound for Fort William, Ontario (now

Thunder Bay) on Lake Superior. Like many of his colleagues, her captain apparently ignored the posted storm warnings. Regardless of the weather, he would plow through it. He had a schedule to keep. After he passed Harbor Beach, Michigan, on Lake Huron during the late morning of Saturday, November 9, the strong west wind started to quickly shift, going first southeast then northeast and ending up north-northeast. All the while the wind ominously increased in strength.

By about 3:00 p.m. the *Hanna* was off Point Aux Barques, Michigan, and struggling to keep her bow into the malignant waves. Even with full power, she could barely make headway. Huge waves swept down her decks and the pumps were going constantly to keep the bilges clear.

At 6:30 p.m. the beating the waves were giving the ship began to show results. The starboard oiler's door was smashed in and minutes later two engine room doors and windows were gone. Down in the engine room the men were soon laboring in knee-deep water and more was coming in all the time. An hour later the ship began to literally come apart. The cook's room and dining room were swept away, woodwork torn from the walls and washed down into the engine room along with tables, chairs and cookware. The engineers were shocked to see the cook herself, Sadie Black, come tumbling down the companionway propelled along by a deluge of water. Sadie wasn't very big in stature, weighing just a little over a hundred pounds, but she picked herself up and climbed back up to her galley. No wave was going to wash her away from her duty station!

The *Hanna* continued to be ripped apart by the storm. The pilothouse doors and windows were shattered and roof ripped off by the waves. The forward men huddled from the storm in the steel Texas deck cabins below the pilothouse. A portion of the stern cabin was swept away as was the smokestack. The crew had lost all idea of where they were. All they knew was the end was near. The steamer could not survive much more of the pounding. Thick snow squalls periodically blotted out visibility.

The 500-foot steel freighter Howard M. Hanna was fast on Point Au Barques Reef. Stonehouse Collection.

Just before 10:00 p.m., the men still clinging to the bridge saw the beam of Port Austin Light and knew they were very close to the dangerous reef. Against all odds, the crew was able to drop both bow anchors in the hope they would catch and hold the steamer off the reef. The attempt failed. Either the anchors didn't bite into the rocky bottom, or the force of the seas just bounced them along the sand. Within minutes, the HANNA hit the reef broadside. The tortured steel of the hull howled in protest as she was driven hard on the rocks. Within minutes she was listing to starboard and the grasping waves were starting to tear off her hatch covers.

The pilothouse crew was trapped forward while the rest of the 25-person crew were trapped in the stern. The seas sweeping along the open spar deck prevented any movement between the two groups.

While the crew huddled in fear and prayed for salvation, Sadie went to work doing what she did best, cook. She managed to get a fire going in her galley stove and in spite of waist-deep water in both galley and messroom, she kept the men in the stern supplied with piping hot coffee and what food the lake had not swept away. When the storm finally moderated a bit on Monday, she was able prepare some hot food. The mate struggled forward with a ration for the men trapped there. It was the first they had eaten in nearly two days.

On Tuesday the forward men made their way aft and noticed a large crack across the spar deck at the Number Seven Hatch. The vessel was actually breaking in two. Both life rafts and one lifeboat were also missing, washed away by the storm seas.

The crew fired distress rockets to attract attention but didn't know if anyone saw them. About 8:30 Monday morning the U.S. Life Saving Service lookout at Port Austin had sighted the ship on the reef, about three miles to the northwest and a mile and a half off shore. The lifesaving crew was unable to immediately help. The storm had destroyed both their boathouse and dock and seriously damaged their boats. They telephoned nearby stations for help, but those stations were deeply committed to their own rescues. Port

Austin would have to do the best they could. The lifesavers took the least damaged of their boats, a spare surfboat and launched it for the wreck. After going barely half-mile, the boarding seas and water flooding in through numerous leaks in the hull, made it unmanageable and they had to return to shore. The lifesavers dug a second surfboat out from the wrecked boathouse but discovered its gunwale was broken in five places, and there were several holes in the bottom. Quickly, they went to work patching the boat. By next morning temporary repairs were made and they launched for the wreck.

Meanwhile back on the *Hanna*, the crew were desperate to get off the wreck and on Tuesday morning nine of the men launched the single remaining lifeboat and headed for the shore. The seas were still running high but the sailors were able to safely land on the beach.

When the lifesavers reached the steamer they took six of the crew including Sadie into their boat. Sadie refused to be treated any differently than any of the men. She left the ship in the order she felt was proper. She was in a poor way when she finally entered the bouncing surfboat. The days of exposure to the icy water and freezing temperatures had badly wracked her small frame. The storm warriors were concerned the cook would die before reaching shore. The surfboat was leaking heavily and was likely floating on her internal air tanks. All aboard were sitting in water and bailing for all they were worth. Once ashore the local residents took the shipwreck victims into their homes where they were fed and warmed. The lifesavers made another run to the wreck and safely brought the remainder of the crew ashore.

The plucky cook had lost all of her possessions when her cabin washed away, including clothes, jewelry and $150 in cash. The crew however, in appreciation of her tenacity and dedication, collected a purse for her.

While most of the crew eventually returned to sail the lakes again, for Sadie and Clarence it was their last trip. They never sailed again.[13]

CHAPTER THREE

THE CAPTAIN WAS A SHE

CAPTAIN IN PETTICOATS

One of the least traditional jobs a woman held on the lakes a century ago was that of ship's captain. It just wasn't done. The ones that did manage to do it were rarer than "hen's teeth." Celia E. Persons was one of this select group.

Celia E. Parsons was one of the earliest licensed lake captains. US Life Saving *Service Heritage Association.*

She was born in Bath, Summit County, Ohio, and attended Oberlin College near Cleveland. In 1872, she took a position teaching music in Alpena, Michigan, on the shores of Lake Huron. There the young Ohioan met a handsome surfman from the Thunder Bay Island Life Saving Station. After a quick courtship, she and John Persons were married. Soon after the wedding John was appointed keeper of the station.

Thunder Bay Island is located three miles east of Alpena, at the entrance to Thunder Bay. By accompanying John to and from the station in various small boats, Celia learned to sail and navigate around the many treacherous reefs and shoals. Under her husband's expert instruction, she became an accomplished sailor in fair weather or foul.

As the wife of the keeper, Celia also had the unofficial duty of ministering to the various needs of many shipwrecked sailors her husband and his crew saved. Many times when John and his crew were performing a dangerous rescue, she nervously waited ashore with hot coffee and warm blankets. Doubtlessly she would have remembered the April 1879, disaster at Point aux Barques, farther south on the Lake Huron shore. Keeper Jerome Kiah and his men headed out in their surfboat in the midst of a strong gale to go to the aid of a schooner thought to be in distress. Crossing the outer bar, the boat capsized. In the pounding waves the men righted it several times, only to tumble again and again. When the day was done, Kiah was the only survivor. The other seven men of his crew had died. Celia knew the lifesavers motto "Regulations say we have to go out. They don't say anything about coming back." Celia stood loyally on the shore, waiting to help in any way she could. One local paper stated she acted as a nurse to "the blackest fireman, the ordinary deckhand and the master of a steamer–all looked alike to her–human beings in distress."

During the quiet summer weather when tourists visited the island, she played the role of "genial hostess," welcoming all to her home with a smile. It was said sailors and lifesavers all along the lakes knew her.

John saw the need for a steamer and, being an accomplished boat builder, set about making one. Within a short time, he had built the steam yacht *Florence C.*, launching her in 1889. He took out the required papers to become her engineer. But Celia one-upped him. She studied for and passed the difficult master's exam! When the yacht steamed in and about Thunder Bay, it was Celia at the wheel. Later she captained the steamer *Marcia*. She had added a Capt. to her Mrs!

A local paper commented on the lack of female masters on the lakes. "The captain of the steam yacht *Emma G.* of Cleveland is a lady. There is we believe, a young woman on the Mississippi possessing a master's papers and another on the Ohio." Another was 16-year-old Lillian McGowan, who was said to have mastered a 600-ton Great Lakes lumber schooner.

There were other women skippers, too–in fact if not in name. There was a brig that sailed out of Port Burwell on the Canadian side of Lake Erie with an interesting management team. The ship

"Under a firm hand." Stonehouse Collection.

was owned by a family consisting of a mother, father and son. The nominal captain was the father with the son holding down the mate's billet. The mother managed the vessel, hiring the crew, paying the wages and collecting the freight money.

Whenever the father became "lit," which was often, the mother would throw him on to the beach and tell the son to "single up your lines, mister, and get sail on her!" The son would ask, "What course, maw?" She would reply, "For Cleveland, or Detroit" whatever the case was. Then she'd tell him to "lay out the course yourself." The son would yell to the man at the wheel, "sou-sou'west and no higher," or whatever he wanted.

That it was the mother who sailed the brig was no doubt. She kept it rolling along in fair weather or foul. When the husband eventually sobered up and rejoined the ship, she berated him for his weakness, then stepped back as he again assumed the quarterdeck.

If either father or son ran her aground or damaged the rigging, the mother would take the repair money out of their "cut" of the profits. There was never any doubt that the lady was the real "master." Regardless of these examples, women captains on the lakes were, indeed very rare.

Celia Persons, an educator, lifesaver's wife and vessel captain, was a woman far ahead of her time. She didn't worry about what women "didn't" do, she just did it!

Celia was with John for 19 years of his Life Saving Service career. When she died, the local paper was moved to comment she was "one of the greatest lifesavers on the Great Lakes." It further said she was "the best beloved woman of the Service." Floral tributes arrived at the Alpena Congregational Church from all over the lakes. Not only did lifesavers come from Lake Huron stations at Middle Island, Tawas, Harbor Beach and Sturgeon Point, all relatively close come to the funeral, but also men from Vermilion Point and Two-Hearted River on distant Lake Superior. [14]

CAPTAIN BUCKLEY AND THE *FANNY CAMPBELL*

A genuine woman captain of an old wind wagon was Maud Buckley. Born in Wellington County, Ontario, in 1864, at age 17 she married Captain Thomas Gillies of Kincardine, Ontario. Their marriage lasted long enough for Maud to deliver two young sons before her husband died on the lake. He was standing on top of the cabin of the schooner *Annie Watt*, when she came about in a stiff breeze and the boom knocked him into the water where he drowned.

With a husband gone and children to care for, she had to earn her own living, so Maud sailed as a cook in several lake schooners, as had many sailor widows. In time, she married one of her captains, James Buckley. After sailing for years with her husband in the schooner *Fanny Campbell*, she became very experienced in handling the ship., During one trip when he fell ill, she took the ship safely into port. His illness was a debilitating one and when it was apparent he would never sail again, she, in the expression of the times, "wrote the examination" and received her captain's papers. The *Fanny Campbell* was the family livelihood and keeping it a going concern was important.

The 404-ton schooner was built in 1868, by Shickluna at St. Catharine's, Ontario. In 1877, $10,000 was spent to construct large iron tanks in the hull for carrying oil cargoes. Whether the tanks remained for the ships entire career is unknown.

Once she had her papers, Captain Buckley hired another woman as cook and a crew of a mate and six seamen. By any measure, she skippered the *Fanny Campbell* as efficiently as any male captain. It was said she was as "quick as a cat" and went aloft to the topsail yards if needed. Nor was she ever beaten to the weather earring of an upper topsail when it was needed to shorten or make sail.

Captain Buckley was also refined and well-mannered. She invariably wore a skirt, never trousers, unless the job called for it. Neither did she drink, smoke or swear. Like most sailors of the period, she also thought women smoking cigarettes was ridiculous.

Shipwreck on Lake Michigan.

Shipwreck on the lakes, a schooner in the breakers. Stonehouse Collection.

Captain Buckley sailed the *Fanny Campbell* for a number of years, until she finally wrecked in a fierce Lake Huron gale in the fall of 1899. The circumstances of loss are generally unknown, but it is likely that she was caught in a northeast gale strong enough to shred her sails. Driven by the wind, she went into the breakers two miles south of Harbor Beach, Michigan.[15]

The local lifesaving crew brought their lifeboat alongside the schooner and the keeper yelled to the woman at the rail to jump for it. Imagine his surprise when he heard a woman's voice singing above the crashing waves, "I'm captain of this vessel and I'll be the last to leave. Come on down from aloft boys and jump as you all see your chance." Every crewmen obeyed the captain's order. When all were safe in the lifeboat, Captain Buckley grabbed the fall of the mizzenboom topping-lift, swung out and dropped easily into the tossing lifeboat.

Captain Buckley never commanded another vessel. Her husband had died in the meantime, so she took a job as a cook on the steamer *Edmonton* running between Sarnia and Port Arthur. She cooked on the *Edmonton* for a dozen years.

She was remembered as being generous to a fault and spent most of her money helping destitute sailors. Captain Buckley died in March 1936 at age 80 in Port Huron, Michigan, after a month's illness.[16]

SCHOONER YACHT UNDER WAY, SHOWING ALL PLAIN (WORKING) SAIL SET.

Fred. S. Cozzens
86

1. Foretopmast or Jib Topsail Stay.
2. Flying Jibstay.
3. Jibstay.
4. Forestay.
5. Flying Jib.
6. Jib.
7. Forestaysail.
8. Fore Gaff Topsail.
9. Foresail.
10. Maintopmast Staysail.
11. Main Gaff Topsail.
12. Mainsail.
13. Jib Topsail furled on Jib Boom.
14. Jib Boom.
15. Bowsprit.
16. Martingale.
17. Fore and Main Shrouds rattled down.
18. Bobstays, which secure the Bowsprit and prevent it from lifting.

Knowing the rigging of a schooner was a daunting task. Stonehouse Collection.

GRACE WAITE

In 1906, a Grace Waite of Toledo became the first woman in the Toledo Steamboat Inspection Service District to be licensed as a pilot. In June of that year, Grace appeared in the office of the Steamboat Inspector Service and took the written captain's exam. Successfully passing, it proved her knowledge of seamanship, navigation, pilot rules, whistle and bell signals, use of compass and charts and the location and characteristics of lights, lighthouses and buoys.

Captain Waite was licensed to run between Toledo and Port Clinton, a distance of approximately 30 miles. She was also limited to commanding gasoline freight boats not exceeding 25 gross tons and not carrying passengers.

She was the wife of George R. Waite, the owner and engineer of the *Naomi*, a small coast trading vessel. The *Naomi* was 56 feet in length and 22 gross tons. During the summer it carried produce from the country ports to the city. Grace demonstrated her expertise to the steamboat inspectors by proving four years of work as a wheelsman, one year in the sailboat *Pathfinder*, one year in the gasoline boat *Piscatory* and two years in the *Naomi*.

Mastering the small *Naomi* wasn't like being captain of a 600-foot freighter, but it was a step up the ladder from the galley. It would be a long time yet, but sometime they would be deck officers on the great commercial fleets running the length of the Great Lakes.[17]

SARAH CLOW

Although Sarah Clow never captained a vessel, there is little doubt that she could have done it. Sarah was the wife of Captain David Clow, well-known in the Door Peninsula on the Wisconsin side of Lake Michigan, as a shipbuilder and captain. Throughout his career he built numerous sail craft and mastered others. One of his greatest building exploits was the schooner *Sarah Clow* as related in the *Detroit Free Press* of August 11, 1868.

A fine new bark of 500 tons burden was launched at Chamber's Island, on the 30th ult. She was built by the owner, David Clow. She is 155 feet long, 31 feet wide and 11 feet hold. In alluding to this launch, it may be proper to mention the energy and perseverance displayed by Mr. Clow and his better half in their experience of ship-building, and the following narrative from the *Green Bay Advocate* will be found interesting.

"The mere launching of a vessel, in this country, where launches are so common, is usually a subject of but a passing brief paragraph. But here is one which demands something more. And here let us go back a few years, and look at the history of this David Clow, for we are proud to point him out as a Wisconsin man and the very emolument of the spirit of western enterprise, and with his wife, who is in reality a "help-make" as well as "help-mate," nine years ago conceived the idea of building a vessel.

"To this undertaking they both spend their entire energies, husband and wife together actually sawing out the planking by hand with a whip saw. The two built her entirely, from stem to stern and from keel to truck, built her almost entirely without iron, pinning her together with wooden trunnels–and the proud result–after seven years of toil, the schooner *Sarah Clow*. She proved to be a strong, seaworthy vessel, and during six or eight years she has been in service, has realized a rich reward for her energetic builders and owners.

"Once indeed, she was supposed to be lost, and here again Capt. Clow's energy was brought into notice. In a storm she was driven ashore, across a

tongue of land and into a sort of inland pond some distance from the lake, where there was no water sufficient to float her. The insurance company gave her up, but Clow did not. He actually cut a channel for her, and worked her out to the lake with a windlass in safety. And now his second vessel, the *Lewis Day*, named in honor of our townsman, floats upon the bay. May she be as fortunate as the first, and may he and his wife long live to enjoy the prosperity they have so nobly won."[18]

"I'M NOT MOVING"

Louise Talbot of the schooner *Sunshine* was cut from the same cloth as Maud Buckley of the *Fanny Campbell*. The following article from the July 30, 1903, *Detroit Free Press* demonstrates her tenacity in fighting for her rights.

> "Find me a dock or a cargo and I'll get out of your way in a hurry," [said] Louise Talbot, captain, mate, engineer, pilot, cook, deckhand, stewardess, crew, in fact about everything–but owner of the schooner *Sunshine* paused long enough in her work of applying coat of pale blue paint to the cabin roof of the weather beaten old craft which lay at the waterworks dock, yesterday afternoon to hand down the above ultimatum to Capt. Bullock of the schooner *Selkirk*, coal laden, which was lying nearby, waiting for an opportunity to get into the canal which leads to the pumping station, and whose progress was blocked by the *Sunshine*.
>
> That ultimatum, furnished by a lone woman, marked the culmination of a day's warfare that was as unique as it was exasperating to the captain of the

Selkirk, and when darkness fell the plucky little woman was still in possession of the channel, the craft guarding it still being tied securely to the dock, while the captain of the other vessel paced up and down and swore in several languages.

An interesting character is Louise Talbot, sailor of many years experience, who is equally at home in the galley or at the wheel, who can splice a rope as deftly as she can fry fish, and whose accomplishments in the nautical line are limited only by the opportunities which the weather-beaten old schooner furnish her. She was busily engaged in painting the roof of the cabin yesterday afternoon, but dropped brush and bucket long enough to tell of her troubles.

Some weeks ago the *Sunshine*, which is at present under a cloud, and whose brightest days were passed many years ago, brought a cargo of coal to the pumping station. After that there was "nothing doing," no cargo being available, and the boat, in order to save expense, was anchored at the water works dock, on the west side, and directly in the channel leading to the canal.

"The *Selkirk*, hailing from Lorain, came along in a few days with a cargo of coal and the *Sunshine* was moved long enough to let her get in and unload. Again was this performance repeated. Gradually, the crew of the *Sunshine* dwindled until Captain Bullock again arrived with the *Selkirk* from Sandusky yesterday morning, he found the woman in sole possession, and the boat back in the channel.

In vain did he appeal to Supt. Starkey, to Chief Engineer Gould, and to everyone else within reach, but whose combined persuasive powers proved ineffectual. The plucky woman declared that she had hunted from one end of the town to the other in an effort to find a dock at which to tie, and as none was forthcoming there was nothing to do but stay where she was. And that appeared to be the only alternative, for the towing powers of the *Selkirk* were as inadequate as were the propelling powers of the *Sunshine*. The channel at the waterworks dock is just wide enough to allow one vessel to pass through at a time, and the *Sunshine* lays directly in the course which the *Selkirk* would have to take.

"If only I could find a dock or cargo I'd be alright," said the Talbot woman, who in addition to her other multifarious duties is acting as general manager for the craft. "But I've looked for both until I'm tired out. I guess the only thing to do will be to get a tug and be towed out in the stream and anchor there until something turns up."

In an effort to retain her hold on the present anchorage, the woman telephoned the corporation counsel's office yesterday afternoon, but was informed that as no rent was being paid, she had no claim on the dock. Meanwhile Capt. Bullock frets and fumes and swears vengeance, and threatens to do desperate things to the *Sunshine* and everyone connected with her.

There is no record of the how exactly the standoff finally worked out, but with a captain of Louise Talbot's character, she assuredly came out of the fracas with her rights intact![19]

Several women captained Great Lakes schooners during the heyday of sail. Stonehouse Collection.

CHAPTER FOUR
SKIRTS IN THE TOWER

FIRST KEEPER

The first female keeper on the Great Lakes was Rachel Wolcott at Marblehead, Ohio. She was the wife of the first keeper, Benajah Wolcott, appointed in 1822, when the light was first placed in operation. After he died at age 68 on August 11, 1832, she was appointed in his place. Supposedly, he died as the result of contracting cholera from helping to bury victims of the dreaded disease. His son died at about the same time, likely of the same cause.

Marblehead Lighthouse. US Coast Guard.

Rachel of course had to take care of not only the light, but also her home, garden and related livestock, and family. Her two children by Benajah, Henry and Elizabeth, were five or six years old, so were of little help. It is possible one or more of Benajah's children from his first marriage may have helped Rachel in her numerous responsibilities.

The lighthouse illuminating apparatus was the old Lewis equipment, consisting of an incredibly inefficient combination of lamps, reflectors and lenses. Maintaining it was difficult at best. In addition, she had to polish all the brasswork, sweep and clean the walls, balconies, stairs, floors and related areas. It was a never-ending job. Before marrying Benajah, Rachel had been a schoolteacher in Sandusky. Her life at the lighthouse, far out on the sparsely populated point, must have been a lonely one.

Her tenure as lightkeeper and widow was short. In less than two years she had married Jeremiah Van Benschoten. He was appointed keeper in her place on February 14, 1834 and kept the light for eight years.

The number of female lightkeepers varied through the years. In 1877, there were 143 United States Great Lakes lighthouses. Seven were manned by women keepers and 18 had female assistants.

The pioneering work done by Thomas and Phyllis Tag in their five-volume set of Great Lakes lighthouse keepers has been instrumental in trying to come to grips with the question of how many female lighthouse keepers there were on the Great Lakes?"[20] Although their data is admittedly not 100 percent accurate due to missing information, it is none-the-less a groundbreaking compilation of Great Lakes lightkeepers, their dates of assignment, and stations.

The volumes reveal just how rare female keepers were. There were 43 female keepers and 63 assistants–for a total of 106. Compared to the roughly 3,445 male keepers, approximate-

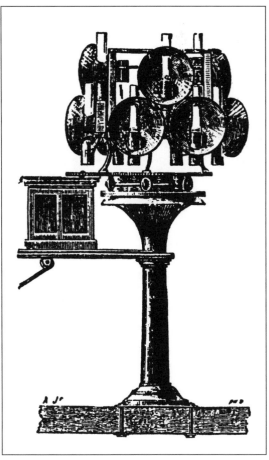

The Lewis Lamp system was difficult to maintain and operate. Stonehouse Collection.

ly only 3 percent of the lighthouses were operated by female keepers. Of the 43 keepers, 17 held the position for less than a year, and 22 replaced their husbands, invariably as the result of his death or incapacitation. Of the 63 assistant keepers, 49 were assistants under their keeper husbands.

The point of this quick analysis is to clearly show that female keepers or assistants were very rare, and that the majority only achieved their positions through their husband's coattails. It was definitely not a level playing field.

As the numbers show, the women achieved their appointments by being the daughters or wives of keepers who died "in the saddle." In effect, they received "sympathy" positions. There were exceptions. Harriet Colfax in Michigan received her appointment purely through politics, her cousin being Schuyler Colfax, the Vice President of the United States (1869-73) under President Ulysses Grant.

Even when a husband-keeper died, women usually faced stiff competition for their positions. After the death of keeper Barney Litogot at Mamajuda Light in the Detroit River in 1873, the assistant keeper applied for the job. But since the assistant keeper was also his wife and a number of men wanted the position, it took the intervention of the district superintendent to secure it for her. In his letter to the Secretary of the Treasury, he pointed out she had actually kept the light for years because her Civil-War-veteran-husband was too much of an invalid to perform his duties. Caroline Litogot held the job until her resignation in 1885.

There was a story that in 1891, the keeper of Marquette Light managed to have his wife appointed as his assistant. The following year he asked to her "unappointed," having discovered that the work of the light wasn't being done. In a traditional lighthouse the keeper and his assistants–if he had any–took care of the light, lenses, lamps, machinery and other heavy work about the station. The wife took care of keeping the house and other family requirements. The lighthouse inspector checked the work of each. With his wife as assistant keeper, the family faced the quandary of

Operating and maintaining the big steam fog signals was considered too difficult for women keepers. Stonehouse Collection.

what job to do–that of wife or that of assistant keeper? One of them would surely suffer. The solution was for the keeper to hire someone to do the assistant's job, which meant he had no financial gain from his assistant keeper-wife.

The appointment of women as keepers or assistant keepers at isolated stations was also discouraged. The officials felt women were not as capable in the event of accident. Considering the Victorian ideal of a woman–someone who lived for her husband's pleasure, to manage the household but keep demurely in the background–this was sound reasoning.

The 1948 issue of the *Coast Guard Bulletin* offered an explanation for the decline of woman lightkeepers. While the thoughts expressed are hardly "politically correct" in today's point of view, it was the reasoning of the time.

In days gone by, the duties and lives of these woman keepers were often arduous in the extreme, but principally because of the great isolation of the sites on which many lighthouses were built, and the lack of modern convenience. These women often performed acts of heroism, not unexpected where they lived so surrounded by the sea: and on numerous occasions made personal sacrifices that the signals under their charge might not fail the mariners.

It was the development of steam fog signals and their coal fired boilers, and the later introduction of heavy internal combustion engines, which first placed the duties of keepers of lighthouses beyond the capacity of most women. Their gradual retirement from this field of employment was further hastened when intricate electrical equipment was placed at many stations, and when the duties of lighthouse keepers gradually came to require special training and when many of the newer stations were built offshore on submarine foundations. As these changes took place, those women who remained in the Lighthouse Service were transferred to or were retained at stations where the equipment was of a more simple type. Soon still other developments and inventions were to invade the world of the woman keeper, for in those quiet backwaters, where comparatively primitive equipment was still found adequate, it was found that automatic apparatus could be effectively substituted, and many smaller lighthouses were converted into automatically operated stations or made parts of groups of lights tended by keepers who maintained a patrol by means of smaller boats. These changes practically closed the lighthouse field to women.

Elizabeth Whitney Williams. US Coast Guard.

ELIZABETH WILLIAMS OF BEAVER ISLAND

"I was called from a sound sleep by my mother saying, 'Get up quick Elizabeth, there is the vessel at anchor just in front of our house.' …Father and John were carrying goods to the shore, the captain and another man were loading the yawl, mother and I carried what we could.…All was loaded except a few boxes and two large trunks. When father and John started to go back to the shore after them several [men] were standing besides the goods and each had a gun in his hands. This was enough. Father knew that the rest of our goods must be left. Our sails were quickly hoisted, the

79

anchor pulled up and soon we were sailing toward Charlevoix.... The sun was just coming up in the east and as we looked back we could see the door of our house stood open as our doors had always been to strangers or any who needed help. None had ever gone away cold or hungry. And some of the people who now stood on the shore with guns pointed toward us had been fed and cared for by my people."[21]

With these words, Elizabeth Williams recorded in her book, *A Child of the Sea; and Life Among the Mormons*, how she and her family were driven away by the Mormons in the dead of night and at the point of a gun from their Beaver Island home. It was certainly a terrifying experience for a young girl.

Williams' writings of Beaver Island provide one of the best records available of this tumultuous period of Great Lakes history. At the time, Beaver Island was very much at the edge of the American frontier and the ragged edge of civilization. Justice could be quick and rough, as the eventual fate of the Mormons clearly showed.

Elizabeth Williams later became one of the most famous female lightkeepers of the Great Lakes. Her early childhood was spent on St. Helena Island in northern Lake Michigan where her father found employment as a ship's carpenter. From there the family moved to Beaver Island, 32 miles to the southwest, where he worked for a time as a commercial fisherman.

Her unique book provides a first hand look at the stormy Mormon period on Beaver Island. This small offshoot of the Mormon religion was organized by Jesse James Strang after the death of the founder, Joseph Smith. Strang was a charismatic leader. Born in New York State, he had been a teacher, lawyer and postmaster before finding his calling as a prophet of Mormonism. In the confusion following Smith's death, Brigham Young and Strang fought for the leadership of the group. Strang had been a Mormon for merely five months when he tried to seize control, which certainly lessened his creditability. Young eventually won the struggle and led most of the members to Utah. In 1848, Strang took

Jesse James Strang, the self appointed "King of Beaver Island."
Stonehouse Collection.

a much smaller group to Beaver Island with the hope of founding a colony in the isolation offered by its remote location. Beaver Island is about 13 miles long and six wide, and is 24 miles off the mainland of Michigan. There is evidence that prehistoric mound builders once used the island, but when French explorers arrived in the mid-17th century, the Ojibway occupied it. When Strang arrived, however, the inhabitants were traders and fishermen. Strang called his followers "Saints" and non-believers "Gentiles."

His reception on the island was generally negative. The inhabitants knew the history of the Mormons was filled with conflict, and having a group on the island who thought themselves to be God's chosen people was uncomfortable to those who were not of the Mormon faith. Friction with the islanders was constant and arose over land, fishing, trade and the Saints peculiar beliefs, especially polygamy. This last belief deeply offended traditional Christian values. Strang alone had four wives and 14 children! Initially the Saints were a bothersome minority to the Gentiles. Over time, more and more of them reached the island. By 1850, seventy-four percent of the population were Saints, and at the spring election they gained the majority of offices–much to the chagrin of the Gentiles. Eventually, more than 2,000 Saints would inhabit the island.

On July 8, 1850, Strang had himself ceremoniously crowned "king" of Beaver Island. He also claimed he had a revelation that "...God gave the islands of the Great Lakes to the Saints." This neatly solved any land problems with the Gentiles, since all of the land now belonged to the Saints–regardless of deeds or other minor legal documents. Although the proper authorities took a dim view of such "revelations," they took no effective action to enforce applicable land titles.

Succumbing to Strang's relentless pressure and intimidation, the remaining Gentiles fled the island, abandoning their homes and businesses. Williams' family was among the last refugees to flee the Saints. Strang had given them 10 days to either convert to the Saints or leave the island. For the beleaguered islanders, it was no choice at all. The family first settled at Charlevoix and later, Traverse City.

Rightly or wrongly, Strang's band gained a reputation for thievery and piracy. Some Gentiles referred to them as a "band of forty thieves" or "Society of the Illuminati," who sailed boats ready to assault any lakeside town should they discover the men gone and families left unprotected. Once, when some Gentile fishermen were driven ashore on Beaver Island by a storm, a group of Saints suggested killing them outright. After much discussion, they were just robbed and set adrift.

Perhaps surprisingly, Strang took an active role in establishing lighthouses. He lobbied hard for two on Beaver Island, at St. James Harbor and Beaver Head on the south end, to make the island more attractive to steamships to stop and buy his colony's cordwood. Although very clannish, the Saints needed trade to generate hard currency. It is ironic that Strang, for whom Elizabeth Williams had a profound dislike, was instrumental in obtaining the St. James Lighthouse she so loved.

By virtue of his election to the Michigan Legislature, representing his Saint–dominated district, Strang was able to arrange for one of his men to be appointed keeper of the Aux Galets Lighthouse (Skillagalee), a small island east of Beaver Island. Once the Saints keeper took over, lake captains complained that the man would turn off the tower light and display false ones in an effort to entice vessels onto the rocks and shoals so they could be plundered by the Saints. Such charges must have angered Williams, who later became a dedicated lightkeeper.

Old lake sailors told stories of vessels disappearing in the vicinity of Beaver Island in mid-summer, and that neither they or their crews were ever heard of again. It was expected that some vessels would "go missing" in the fall, but it was nearly unheard of in the summer. The sailors claimed the Mormons boarded the vessels, killed the crews, stole the cargos and then burned or scuttled the ships to assure there was no evidence. Dead men told no tales about Beaver Island.

Strang's heavy-handed leadership rankled many of the Saints. Some refused to follow his increasingly stringent dictates. For example, when he issued a dress code for women requiring a sort of bloomer costume, many balked at following it. When Mrs. Thomas Bedford refused to wear the bloomers, Strang had her husband publicly whipped. Bedford and another man, whose wife also refused to wear the costume, plotted revenge. Luring Strang from his house they ambushed him near the boat dock with a fusillade of bullets. Several loyal Saints took the mortally wounded prophet to his old home in Vorees, Wisconsin. After lingering for a while, on July 8, 1856, he died, six years to the day after crowning himself "king."

With Strang off the island and dying, retribution against the Saints was swift. A group of 50-80 armed Gentiles descended on the island between July 5-6, 1856, and with the fire of holy vengeance in their eyes! The Saints were driven onto ships waiting in the harbor and taken to Detroit or Chicago. The unfortunates lost nearly all their processions, not unlike the Gentiles when Strang drove them away. The Gentiles' reoccupied the island, taking over the abandoned Saints' homes as they had stolen the Gentiles property years before. Williams' family was among those returning. The man who led the vigilante group was A.P. Newton, a businessman from St. Helena Island, Michigan. This was the same A.P. Newton who would later receive the government contract in 1870 to build the new tower in St. James and make other lighthouse improvements. In this regard, Williams would have worked closely with him.

Elizabeth evidently met her first husband, Clement Van Riper, on the island. He had come there from Detroit in an attempt to recover his health. Initially he operated a large cooper shop at the point making barrels for the fishing industry. Shipping fish required barrels, making their manufacture a key component to the industry. In 1862, he received an appointment as the government schoolteacher to the Indians on Garden Island, just to the north of Beaver

The white picket fence provided a homey touch to the St. James Light. US Coast Guard.

Island. The teaching position lasted two years and mostly involved instruction in agricultural methods. By 1865, Williams and her husband left Beaver Island, living first at Northport and later at Charlevoix, Michigan. When the keeper of Harbor Point

Lighthouse, Peter McKinley, resigned in 1869, her husband was appointed to the position in his place. McKinley had earlier operated the trading post on Whiskey Point, which, as it sold whiskey and was a gathering place for disgruntled Gentiles, drew Strang's special ire. Elizabeth and her husband devoted their full attention to making the lighthouse a success. Not only did she keep house, but also took the time to learn how to keep the light. In this regard she served as an unofficial assistant keeper

The original lighthouse, as advocated by Strang, was built in 1856 to help guide ships into St. James harbor for shelter from storms. The light was visible for nine miles. As Strang had hoped, many steamers also stopped to purchase cordwood. A taller tower was erected in 1870, and at the same time other improvements made to the dwelling, including a new brick kitchen. A new fourth order Fresnel lens was also added. Today, only the lonely tower remains, the dwelling having been torn down many years ago.

When her husband Clement became ill, much of the work of keeping the light fell on Elizabeth's shoulders. Maintaining the sparkling lens was her special pride. In her book she noted:

> I took charge of the care of the lamps and the beautiful lens in the tower was my especial care. On stormy nights I watched the light that no accident might happen. We burned the lard oil, which needed great care, especially in cold weather, when the oil would congeal and fail to flow fast enough to the wicks. In long nights the lamps had to be trimmed twice each night and sometimes oftner. At such times the light needed careful watching. From the first the work had a fascination for me. I loved the water, having always been near it and I loved to stand in the tower and watch the great rolling waves chasing and tumbling in upon the shore. It was hard to tell when it was loveliest. Whether in its quiet moods or in a raging foam.

My three brothers were then sailing and how glad I felt that their eyes might catch the bright rays of our light shining out over the waste of waters on a dark stormy night. Many nights when a gale came on we could hear the flapping sails and the captain shouting orders as the vessels passed our point into the harbor, seeking shelter from the storm. Sometimes we could count fifty and sixty vessels anchored in our harbor, reaching quite a distance outside the point, as there was not room for many inside. They lay so close they almost touched at times. At night our harbor looked like a little city with its many lights. It was a pleasant sound to hear all those sailor's voices singing as they raised the anchors in the early morning. With weather fair and white sails set, the ships went gliding out so gracefully to their far away ports. My brothers were sometimes on those ships. Many captains carried their families on board with them during the warm weather. Then what a pleasure to see the children and hear their sweet voices in song in the twilight hours. Then again when they came ashore for a race on land, or taking their little baskets went out to pick the wild strawberries. All these things made life the more pleasant and cheerful.

After Williams returned to the island, the Strang era was like a bad dream. Houses and roads made by the Saints were constant reminders of the dark time when fear ruled the land. While many of their improvements were made use of, she remembered the King's cottage was allowed to go to ruin with some of it carried away as souvenirs by summer visitors.

Captain Henry Bundy and his Gospel ship *Glad Tidings* often called at the island, providing religious services to all. In the early days, there was no doctor. When medical care was needed, one came over from the mainland if it was possible to do so. The mail came by ship via Mackinac Island, 50 miles to the north. Often it was a month or six weeks between deliveries, especially in the winter when the ice had to be solid enough to support a sled. Like keepers at all island stations, it was difficult for Elizabeth to communicate with friends and family. Local farms and fisherman provided a varied diet. In most respects, Beaver Island was a self-contained community. As the lightkeeper's wife, Williams was an integral and important part of it.

Captain Henry Bundy and his schooner Glad Tidings *were frequent visitors to Beaver Island.* Stonehouse Collection.

Tragedy struck early in her marriage. On November 29, 1872, the battered schooner *Thomas Howland* was entering St. James harbor in a sinking condition during a storm. Fearing for the lives of the sailors aboard her, Keeper Clement Van Riper launched a small boat and went bravely to the rescue. What happened in the storm-tossed surf isn't clear, but he and the mate of the schooner were drowned. Neither body was ever recovered. Williams noted in her book "...only those who have passed through the same know what

The schooner Glad Tidings *served as Captain Bundy's floating church. Lake Superior Marine Museum.*

a sorrow it is to lose your loved one by drowning and not be able to recover the remains. It is a sorrow that never ends through life."

The keeper's quarters have been torn down, but the St. James Harbor light tower at Beaver Island still stands. US Coast Guard.

Considering her husband's heroic death, she was appointed lightkeeper in his place. Such a compassionate appointment by the Lighthouse Board was reasonably common during this period. For three years she kept the St. James Light alone. Her father had died earlier and her aged mother was now totally dependent on her for support. Elizabeth was now the breadwinner.

In 1875, she married Daniel Williams, but still remained as keeper. Concerning her appointment, she wrote: "Life to me then seemed darker than the midnight storm that raged for three days upon the deep, dark waters. I was weak from sorrow, but realized that though the life was dearest to me had gone, yet there were others out on the dark and treacherous waters who needed to catch the rays of the shining light from my light-house tower. Nothing could rouse me but that thought, then all my life and energy was given to the work which now seemed was given me to do. The light-house was the only home I had and I was glad and willing to do my best in the Service."

The lakes had not been kind to her. Besides taking her husband, two of three brothers and three nephews were lost at sea. She commented, "…but mine was not the only sorrow. Others around me were losing their loved ones on the stormy deep and it seemed to me there was all the more need that the lamps in our light-house towers should be kept brightly burning."[22]

Perhaps it was during the long winters that she found the time to write her poetry. Considering her personal losses to the grasping lake, her dedication in fact and verse can be understood.

Tribute to The Sailors

Oh sailor boy, sailor boy, sailor boy true!
The lamps in our towers are lighted for you.
Though the sea may be raging your hearts will not fail;
You'll ride through the rolling foam not fearing the gale.

And God in his mercy will lead you aright,
As you watch the light-house with lamps burning bright.
The wind is your lullaby, as the raging seas foam;
Oh sailor boy, sailor boy, we welcome you home.

Oh sailor boy, sailor boy, sailor boy true!
Your sweet darling mother is praying for you;
Your sweet bride is weeping as her vigil she keeps.
Not knowing your ship has gone down into the deep.

As she walks on the shore, her eyes out to sea.
"Oh husband, my sailor boy, come back to me!"
The wild waves dash up at her feet in a foam,
They answer, "Your sailor boy no more can come home."

In sorrow she kneels on that wave-beaten shore,
"Shall I never see my dear sailor boy more?"
The waves whisper softly, their low moaning sound.
"You'll meet your dear sailor boy, in Heaven he's crowned."

Little Traverse Light, circa 1900. Note the fog bell tower. US Coast Guard.

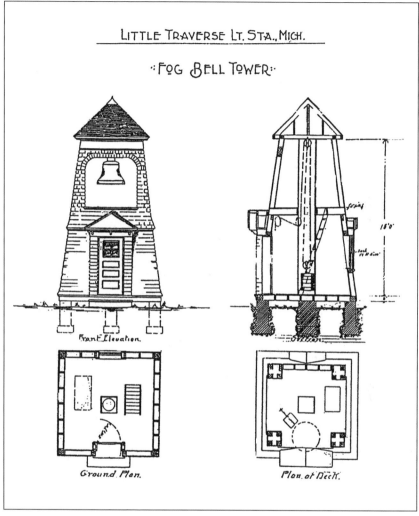

The fog bell tower at Little Traverse Lighthouse is still standing. US Coast Guard.

In 1884, she requested transfer to the new Little Traverse Point Lighthouse on the mainland, 25 miles to the east. The point the lighthouse occupied was also the location of the very exclusive Harbor Point Association, the domain of wealthy families from St. Louis, Chicago and Detroit. Their summer homes were splendid

4. Keepers must be courteous and polite to all visitors and show them everything of interest about the station at such times as will not interfere with light-house duties. Keepers must not allow visitors to handle the apparatus or deface light-house property. Special care must be taken to prevent the scratching of names or initials on the glass of the lanterns or on the windows of the towers. The keeper on duty at the time is responsible for any injury or defacement to the buildings, lenses, lamps, glazing of the lantern and to any other light-house property under his charge, unless he can identify the parties who have done the injury, so as to make them accountable for it; and any such damage must be reported immediately to the inspector or engineer of the district, with the names of the person or persons, if they can be ascertained. No visitor should be admitted to the tower unless attended by a keeper, nor in the watch room or lantern between sunset and sunrise.

Keepers must be courteous to visitors.

The Lighthouse Service's general instruction to lightkeepers required them to be polite to all visitors at the lighthouse.

palaces where the elite of society came to enjoy the north country. There was also a magnificent hotel that catered to the finest guests. Somehow all of them, as well as visitors from the nearby resort communities of Petoskey, Charlevoix and Mackinaw, seemed to find their way to the doorway of the humble lighthouse keeper. Besides wanting to meet this remarkable woman, all desired a personal tour of the grounds and machinery. They were especially interested in the view from high in the tower and workings of the big fog signal. Eventually Williams had to establish a schedule as the only way of accommodating the many visitors and still getting her work done!

The large number of summer tourists was in sharp contrast to the winter desolation. Once the lake froze and snow drifted deep across the roads, life took on a much slower pace. It was time of recuperation, of rest for the long hours needed when the ships again would need her light. At the new light, it was the ships she most longed for. She wrote that, "…[what] I missed the… most was not seeing the passing ships and steamers, as they were constantly passing where we could see them from the island." No matter how busy she was, she always had time to lend a hand in her husband's photography business. Williams kept the Little Traverse Point Light for 29 years, dying on November 3, 1913, at age 71. She had faithfully kept the beacons burning for 41 years at the two lighthouses!

Harriet Colfax, keeper at the Michigan City Light. US Coast Guard.

HARRIET COLFAX AND HER LIGHTHOUSE

While women keepers on the Great Lakes were not unusual, they were not the norm either. For reasons that are not entirely clear, there appears to have been more of them at Michigan City, Indiana, than anywhere else. The most celebrated of all was Harriet Colfax. Her fame encompassed the entire Great Lakes.

As the keeper of the Michigan City Light, she was the proto-typical woman lighthouse keeper on the Great Lakes. She was the

95

standard against which others were measured. When she took over in 1861, she remained on the job until retirement in 1904 at age 80! She was also not the first nor last woman keeper at Michigan City.

The first light to guide arriving ships at Michigan City was a small "post light," a lantern mounted on a tall pole located about 100 feet west of the current lighthouse. Privately maintained, its reliability was suspect and power meager. As commerce increased so did the need for an improved light and, starting in 1834, appropriations were made for a complete lighthouse. Specifications called for a whitewashed 40-foot-tall stone or brick tower with a detached story-and-a-half keeper's house. The light was first exhibited in 1837.

The first keeper was Edmund E. Harrison appointed on December 9, 1837. He was later replaced by Mrs. Harriet E. Tower, the wife of Reverend James Tower, a former principal of a local institute. Her sister, Miss Abigail Coit, acted as assistant keeper. No comments are available concerning the efficiency of the light, but a

Michigan City Lighthouse. US Coast Guard.

contemporary source noted that the women maintained a very tidy house, described in an early report as "…plastered on the outside and dazzling in its whiteness, more of a portico than a veranda ornamented the front and was covered with trailing vines. It fronted south and was surrounded by a grove of small oaks on the west. The well-kept lawn was dotted with shrubbery, flowers and enclosed by a low rustic fence and from a little wicker gate led a white graveled walk to the residence." The sisters kept the light until May 3, 1853, when John Clarkson became the keeper.

As commerce continued to boom, a new and more powerful light was needed. In 1858, the Lighthouse Board built a new lighthouse with a Joliet stone foundation and Milwaukee brick superstructure. The building was quite substantial, with three floors including basement and attic. On the north end the cupola for the lens extended through the roof. A fifth order Fresnel lens provided a beacon visible for 15 miles. If Clarkson anticipated a long tenure in this new building, he was in error.

Although the reasons for Clarkson's departure are not clear, it can be surmised politics played an important part. This was the height of the spoils systems in government. Hiring and firing of personnel, especially in an organization as sensitive to local politics as the Lighthouse Board, was done by political influence. The aftermath of an election meant out with the old keepers and in with the new ones. In this case, Colfax was the new keeper. Her appointment was likely arranged by her cousin, Schuyler Colfax, who, as we have seen, was a powerful congressman who later became vice president under U.S. Grant in 1869. In any case, on March 19, 1861, 37-year-old Harriet E. Colfax was appointed keeper at a salary of $350 per year.

Nothing in her background prepared her for the keeper's job. A more common preparation for a woman keeper was to have been a keeper's wife or daughter, and then to assume the post on his death or disability. Thus, she would be familiar with the full requirements and responsibilities of the position. Colfax came into the position "cold".

She was born in Ogdensburg, New York, in 1824 and had been a voice and piano teacher. She moved to Michigan City in the 1850s with her brother, who founded and published the local newspaper, the *Transcript*. For a while she worked as a typesetter for him and taught music. Some sources talk of a failed romance. Afterwards, she formed a close relationship with a Miss Ann C. Hartwell. She was also an Ogdensburg native who relocated to Indiana to teach school.[23] The two women would spend the rest of their lives together.

Her brother's failing vitality caused him to sell the newspaper and move to a more healthy climate. Colfax remained behind in Michigan City. Perhaps Hartwell influenced her decision.

Colfax was described as a petite and fragile-looking woman. No doubt her appointment raised many eyebrows in the community, especially among men who certainly questioned her ability to do the work. It is also likely Congressman Colfax made no friends on the Lighthouse Board when he forced on them the appointment of an out-of-work female relation. Regardless of how she came to the appointment, Colfax certainly demonstrated a remarkable talent for lighthouse-keeping. By any measure she proved her critics wrong. She kept the light station orderly and clean and ran it "by the book," which helped to slowly defuse local criticism of her appointment.

At the time of her appointment, Michigan City was not a major harbor. *Thompson's Coast Pilot* for 1869 stated there was only five feet of water over the sand bar at the mouth of the harbor. Improvements were needed for the harbor to grow.

Michigan City later had piers on each side of the entrance to the harbor. Proper lighting on the lake ends of the piers was critical to safe navigation. On November 20, 1871, a pierhead light was erected on the east pier, and a 1,500-foot-long elevated walkway from shore to the light provided access. Maintaining the beacon was the responsibility of the Michigan City lightkeeper, in addition to that of the regular shore light.

Stormy Day On Pier. Michigan City Ind.

The Michigan City pierhead was often swept by the waves during storms. US Coast Guard.

Keeping the pier light was a periodic problem for Colfax. Ships entering or leaving the harbor hit the piers regularly, damaging the walkway, sometimes making it difficult if not impossible to reach the light. Reaching the light during storms could be especially dangerous. Imagine the scene: Colfax in a long billowing dress and oil skins trying to work her way down the long, narrow walkway while carrying a container of hot lard oil. The screaming wind would tear at her viciously, threatening to blow the small woman clear off the shaking walkway. Sharp spray from the breaking waves assaulted her constantly. Freezing weather made the walkway treacherous with ice. Slowly, the gallant little woman fought her way along the walkway until she reached the comparative shelter of the beacon. Hopefully, the cold had not caused the lard oil to congeal before she reached the light. If it did, she had to return to the lighthouse, reheat the oil and repeat the entire process. If the oil remained warm enough, when it started to burn it could be kept going from its own radiated heat. When kerosene, known as mineral oil to the keepers, replaced lard oil in July 1880, it must have been a real boon to Colfax as it did not congeal with the cold.

Entries in her official journal cryptically spoke of the difficulty she faced:

> September 18, 1872: Cold day. Heavy N. W. gale towards night. The waves dashing over both piers, very nearly carrying me with them into the lake.
>
> September 29, 1872: Wind blowing westerly gale all day and still rising at 5 p.m. Four vessels entered while the gale was at its height and ran against the elevated walk, breaking it again. Went to the beacon tonight with considerable risk of life.
>
> October 13, 1872: Northerly gale, continuing all day and all night. Weather cold with rain and hail storms. Gale perfectly fearful by nightfall–waves dashed over the top of the beacon–reached the beacon in immanent risk tonight as the waves ran over the elevated walk. Watched

both lights closest attention all night. Wrote to Commander Murray today reporting the trouble I am having with the beacon.

May 28, 1873: A terrible hurricane to-night at about the time of lighting up [the beacon]. Narrowly escaped being swept into the lake.

October 28, 1873: Terrific westerly gale. The waves dashing high over both piers and over my head when on my way down to light the beacon.

Colfax also experienced some difficulty with unwanted visitors. Twice during her tenure, once in 1867 and again in 1891, the situation of intruders settling on the reservation grounds was significant enough to warrant inclusion in the Lighthouse Board's *Annual Report*. She also took note of special events. When General Grant died in July 1885, she was careful enough to drape the lighthouse in black mourning in his honor.

Keeping both lights on the building and pierhead was a very difficult job. Many times she stayed up the entire night nursing them through the darkness. Broken equipment had to be replaced and working gear maintained. Even when the weather cooperated, everything still needed to be cleaned. The work was endless.

Colfax's walkway problems increased markedly in October 1874 when the Lighthouse Board notified her the beacon would be transferred to the west pier, which stood 500 feet farther out into the lake than the east pier. This meant she had to row across Trail Creek, hike along the far shore and then out the longer walkway for the trip out to the light. At times when funds were available she was able to hire an assistant keeper who would live on the west bank to better maintain the outer light. The record is somewhat sketchy, but it appears she had an assistant roughly from November 1871 through May 1873, and thereafter only sparingly.

Regardless of good intentions, sometimes the fury of the lake prevented either Colfax or her assistant from reaching the pierhead light. In these instances, it remained unlit. It was the same when storms carried the walkway away, although on occasion she was able to hire a tug to reach the beacon. She had a narrow escape when a March 1886 storm swept the light off the pierhead and into the lake. Most of the walkway crashed into the water when the light went in. Colfax had only just stepped off the walkway when the disaster happened. With the light gone, she could do nothing until the Lighthouse Board erected a temporary beacon in June.

The impression can be gained that some efforts were made to remove her from the keeper's job. After all, she obtained the position through politics and she could be removed the same way. Perhaps her difficulty in obtaining a permanent assistant could be a subtle way of trying to force a resignation. She was also careful to keep her own political fences mended with congressmen and members of the Lighthouse Board. She did nothing to anger them and everything to keep in their good graces. From this perspective, she, as a politically-appointed female keeper, was no different than a politically-appointed male keeper.

Michigan City Lighthouse was a popular spot for visitors, especially in the summer months. As counseled in the *Instructions for Lightkeepers*, Colfax was a fine and gracious hostess with all her visitors leaving well-pleased with their experience.

Colfax apparently also charmed the various lighthouse inspectors and other official visitors too. They always voiced their complete satisfaction with the lighthouse operation and usually seemed to approve her requests for minor work. Items such as extending the walkway farther back to shore, putting a new floor in the kitchen, and others, made her life considerably easier.

Colfax didn't sequester herself in the lighthouse for 43 years. Occasionally she took leave, especially when an assistant was available. In July 1876, she toured the Centennial Exposition in Philadelphia. In other years she visited friends in Terre Haute, Indiana, and her brother in Wyandotte, Michigan.

Until 1887 the light was attended only during the shipping season, April through November. Starting in 1888, the light was kept the year around. This certainly increased the stress and difficulty Colfax faced.

Although female lightkeepers were excused from heavy work around the station, she had plenty to do in cleaning and polishing the lamps and other implements of lightkeeping. When uniforms were introduced, females were also exempted from the equirement.

In 1894, the Lighthouse Board began recommending in the *Annual Reports* that Michigan City receive a fog signal. Colfax must have viewed such recommendations with some concern, since the adoption would require the kind of heavy labor she was incapable of without a permanent assistant. Moving the hundreds of tons of coal and stoking the voracious boiler fires was very demanding. The fog signal would certainly have threatened her tenure as keeper. As luck would have it, the signal was not installed until after Colfax's retirement.

Her last entry in the station journal was on October 12, 1904. Five months later, on April 16, 1904, she died.

Colfax was not the last of the Michigan City female keepers. Mrs. Julia L. Ebart and Mrs. Katy Reilly both worked as assistants for Colfax in 1872. In sum, there were five female keepers at Michigan City. If this was not a record for the Great Lakes, it certainly is a very impressive showing. [24]

OTHER KEEPERS

There were other female lighthouse keepers on the Great Lakes. Perhaps they were not as well known as Harriet Colfax at Michigan City or Elizabeth Whitney Williams at Beaver Island, but they did their duty to the highest standards of the service and were respected members of their communities.

The story-and-a-half Sand Point Light at Escanaba, Michigan, was built in 1867, at a cost of $11,000. Sited at the end of a long sand spit, its purpose was to guide ships safely past the shallow sand reefs and into the growing iron ore shipping port. Somehow in the construction, the lighthouse was turned 180 degrees, so it is facing land rather than the lake! Luckily for mariners, the tower was effective no matter how it was oriented, so the lighthouse was left as built instead of jacking it up and moving to face the lake.

The first keeper was John Terry. But before the light was finished he died of consumption. His wife, Mary, was appointed in his place. For 18 years she faithfully kept the light, in fair weather or foul. She became a well-respected member of the local community.

Disaster struck early in the morning on Friday, March 4, 1886, when the lighthouse was swept by a terrible fire. When the fire department reached the light at 1:00 a.m., the flames had already broken through the roof, and the insides were a roaring mass of fire. When no one could find Mary, the worst was suspected.

Later, when the fire was out and building cool enough to enter, searchers started the unpleasant tasks of trying to determine the origin of the fire and locate the body of the missing keeper. What was thought to be the remains of Mary were found in the southeast corner of the house, in a room called the oil room. There was very little left–a portion of the skull, a few bones and some viscera. Everything else was consumed by the flames.

The coroner's jury returned a verdict stating that her death was from "causes and means unknown." They believed foul play was involved, but had no evidence. Could it have been a robbery attempt gone bad? At that hour Mary should have been in her bedroom not in the oil room. Did she hear someone in the light and go to investigate, only to be murdered by the intruders? Did they carry her body to the oil room and use the combustibles there as the basis for the fire?

Everyone in town knew Mary was very thrifty and had saved a considerable sum of money from her salary. When the searchers looked through the burned lighthouse they found her hoard in the form of gold coins just where they would have fallen from her cupboard as the fire devoured the wood. Officials thought the door to the light may have been forced open, but they could not be certain. Since the money was still in the light, they also had no motive for

Saginaw River Light, circa 1950. US Coast Guard.

murder. A new keeper was appointed and the light repaired. The mystery of what happened to Mary Terry remains unsolved.

When Peter Brawn, the keeper of the Bay City, Michigan, Light at the entrance to the Saginaw River, became crippled, his wife Julia Toby Brawn assumed his duties. Peter died in 1873, and Julia kept the light until 1890, when her son was appointed keeper.

The Old Mission Point Light on Lake Michigan was kept by Mrs. Sarah E. Lane from December 1906, when her husband died, until July 1908, when a male replacement was appointed.

Mary Ryan was a lightkeeper at the Calumet Pierhead Light near Chicago on Lake Michigan for seven years. From August 7,

Calumet Pierhead Light. Keeper Mary Ryan found it cold and depressing. *US Coast Guard.*

Manitou Island Light in Lake Superior was a lonely and forbidding station.
Stonehouse Collection.

1873, until November 18, 1876, she was the assistant keeper, but from that point until her removal on October 14, 1880, she held the keeper's job. Why she was removed isn't known, but judging from many of her journal entries, she found the job and locale most depressing. She complained it was far too cold for her liking and the summers were never warm enough.

Marquette, Michigan, on Lake Superior was the primary shipping port for iron ore during the Civil War. The coming and goings of the ore freighters was absolutely critical to the war effort. From November 15, 1862, until her removal on October 26, 1865, the keeper of the important Marquette Harbor Light was Eliza Truckey. She replaced her husband, Nelson, who held the position for roughly a year before resigning, most likely for health reasons.

On Lake Huron, Anna Garraty kept the Presque Isle Range Light for 23 years, from 1903-1926. In all weather, Anna was always on the job.

Canadian women also served as keepers. After her keeper-husband died in 1915, Esther Harvey assumed the role as keeper of the Thessalon Light on Lake Huron's Georgian Bay in Ontario. She kept the job for the next quarter century. Vessel masters called her the "brave little lady of the light." Her bravery was tested one day when she heard screams coming from the rocky shore. Running to the sound of danger, she saw a gas boat had run up on the rocks. Acting quickly she saved one man by throwing him her clothesline. The other occupant of the boat had already drowned.

By virtue of the nature of their husband's work, keeper's wives sometimes had incredible experiences. On October 15, 1885, keeper Corgan of the Manitou Island Light near the Keweenaw Peninsula in Lake Superior, wrote in his official logbook: "Principle keeper started 8:00 p.m. in the station boat with wife for Copper Harbor (distant 14 miles) with anticipation of increase soon after arriving. When one and one half miles east of Horseshoe Harbor, Mrs. Corgan gave birth to a rollicking boy; all things lovely, had everything comfortable aboard. Sea a dead calm."[25]

CHAPTER FIVE

ON SHIP AND SHORE

SKIRTS IN THE GALLEY

Being a cook on a Great Lakes vessel might be thought of as a traditional female role. However, in the earliest days of sail women on a ship were considered bad luck and were not willingly carried. There was a practical reason for this taboo. The sailors felt that in a storm, when all hands were needed to work the ship, the "weaker

Cooking for old schooner crews used to be only a man's job. Stonehouse Collection.

sex" would be unable to lend a strong back to the effort. However, the men's desire for good food eventually overcame their prejudice, and women cooks became commonplace.

Working as a cook was, at best, seasonal employment, normally starting in April and running through early November–although the press of business could increase or decrease it. Generally, the cook was hired for the season while the sailors usually only signed on for the trip. The number of female cooks has never been definitely determined. At best the records are spotty but a fair estimate, based on sketchy newspaper reports, would suggest at least a couple of hundred a year from the late 1860s through 1900.

With short trips on the lakes, two weeks at the longest, fresh food was usually not a problem, nor were the number of crew to be fed. A typical schooner might only have a captain, mate and a half-dozen sailors. The requirements of around-the-clock duty for the crew no doubt strained the cook's resources, but not unreasonably.

The female cook was also usually the lowest paid member of the crew. Although a general lack of records precludes making any absolute judgements, there is anecdotal evidence available. In 1873, captains and ship owners met at Kingston, Ontario, and decided male cooks would be paid $30 a month and female cooks $20. Yet this seems to have been wishful thinking. In 1881, a Kingston captain had to pay his female cook $2 a day for the entire season. In 1882, female cooks were receiving $25-$30 monthly, roughly equal to a sailor's pay. The pay for all sailors, cooks included, reflected general economic conditions as well as the law of supply and demand.

Why female cooks were desired over men is hard to explain in retrospective. No doubt it was a combination of reasons. Sometimes they could be employed for less wages than men, thus saving on expenses. In the case of a family-owned ship, the husband being the captain and some relatives crewing, his wife as an unpaid cook could save additional operating cost. There was also the belief that women were "better" cooks than men. Some captains saw an enhanced status to a good-looking female cook

In the 1870s, female cooks were a controversial member of a schooners crew.
Stonehouse Collection.

aboard. It was another way of making his vessel "sharper" than that of a competitor. To this extent, for a while at least, female cooks were a fad. Perhaps there was even an element of sexual fantasy, too! Certainly it was this concern that caused an uproar among some apparently very insecure sailor's wives.

As the following letter from the *Oswego Times* of April 20, 1868, indicates, a fair amount of prejudice developed against the female cooks, usually from sailor's wives. Perhaps there was some truth to their complaints. Most likely it was plain prejudice fired by an overactive imagination. In fact, often the cooks were related to crew members. Sometimes they were the wives of the captains or mates. In situations where the vessel was family owned, her contribution to the success of the business was important, both as a cook and source of presumably unpaid labor.

The issue of male versus female cooks was taken up in this letter which first appeared in the *Buffalo Courier* in 1868, and reprinted in the *Chicago Inter-Ocean.*

A QUESTION FOR LAKE UNDERWRITERS-
MALE VS. FEMALE COOKS.

The *Buffalo Courier* says the following is a literal copy of a letter recently received by a gentleman connected with the Board of Lake Underwriters. There is more truth than poetry–more sound sense than learning–in what the writer says. If we were lake Underwriters we should certainly try and put a stop to the practice alluded to. Playing and fooling with the cook is about the last recreation that a captain should indulge in, and the last that we would be likely to indulge in if that useful functionary was of the male persuasion. But to the letter:

BUFFALO CITY APRIL 14TH 1868

To ——————

Excuse me although a stranger to you—I take the liberty to write you on a subject [which] may interest you. You are aware that very many of our vessel captains are employing woman cooks on their vessels. I would also stated the employment of such cooks is increasing by our Lakemen. Were I the owner of a Vessel I would not allow a woman cook upon my Vessel, for the following reasons. I speak from actual knowledge. I have known two Vessels to be run upon reefs and become almost a total loss for want of a proper officer on deck which mite of prevented such calamity. Question where were the captain and mates? In the cabin Playing fooling with cook. If thar had of been a man cook, it is very likely that his ade would have been cald to assist in managing the Vessel. You may ask what is to be done. Men can be got to due (sic) the cooking for the same wages that is pade to woman cooks. And in case of necesity you have got a man to help work the

Vessel instead of taking the most valuable officer of the vessel to watch the cook instead of the Vessel. You Sir the Board of Marine Underwriters at Cleavland have the means at your disposal to stop this at once by symply saying you will not insure any craft that has got a female cook on by so dueing save a large amount of losses. Now Sir if what I have writen (sic) is worth any thing to you please make best use of it as you in your estimation or judgment may think proper. My statements are facts.

I shall be glad to hear from you if you think it proper to answer me on the subject you can do so by addressing to A. Waterman.

A. Waterman,
Buffalo P.O.

The following April 1883 letter in the *Chicago Inter-Ocean* speaks to the concern of sailor's wives over the unattached female cooks.

Several years ago you brought happiness to many homes along the lakes by driving female cooks off the lakes. Now I want to post you. Captains are sneaking in these women again. They destroy all discipline on shipboard and the assertion by captains to owners that they are cheaper than men cooks and save money to the vessel, is all false. Then in a storm, men cooks can take hold and help, while a woman is only in the way or worse, for she often unnerves the crew by her alarm. Besides all this the mate wants to love the woman cook as well as the captain does and there is often trouble between these two commanding officers. A great grain fleet is about leaving Chicago for below and I want you to drive the women off these vessels. My husband's schooner is among the rest.

For men or women, sailing in the old schooners could be dangerous.
Stonehouse Collection.

There certainly are cases of sailors and cooks becoming "attached" to the chagrin of a lawful spouse as evidenced by the following article from the *Oswego Daily Palladium* (New York) of May 1, 1865.

A Faithless Pair–Last fall, soon after the close of navigation, a man and woman of respectable appearance arrived in this city, and engaged board at the house of a respectable widow lady who resides on the east side of the river. The woman had with her a certificate of membership and good standing, from a church in Detroit, whence the parties came, and were taken into the communion of one of our churches here.

The parties remained at their boarding house during the whole of last winter, and shipped on board a vessel from this port, this spring, the man as mate and the woman as cook. Two or three days after their departure, a woman called upon the lady with whom the mate and cook had been boarding, claimed to be, and in fact had proof that she was, the wife of the mate. She stated that she and her husband had been living in Detroit, and that last fall he left her at that place for the purpose of going to Buffalo to lay up his vessel. She heard nothing further from him, although she had sought him in all the cities along the line of the lakes, till this spring, when in consequence of the information received, she came to Oswego to find that the guilty pair had gone away as stated.

On inquiring of the boarding house keeper, the deserted wife learned that the woman had, and wore valuable articles of jewelry which her husband took away from her when he left her in Detroit. The lady with whom the parties boarded says she will never again take strangers into her house, even if they have certificates of church membership, without certificates of marriage accompanying them. The wife has started for Detroit to head off the gay couple if possible.

Whatever happened when the wife caught up with her husband and his "friend" is not recorded.

On April 29, 1883, a writer in the *Chicago Inter-Ocean* warned of the dangers these cooks faced not from the lake, but from her own shipmates.

> "As a woman, interested in the general welfare of women, I studied up the subject of female cooks on lakes vessels several years ago when the *Inter-Ocean* agitated on the subject and I, with a majority of the ladies of our society, concluded that a single female out at sea, with only men for companions, was in the greatest possible danger, no matter how strong her ideas of right might be. And instances of forced debauchery of a female cook on a sailing vessel are not wanting. Certainly the *Inter-Ocean* has exposed a sufficient number of such cases in the last five years to indicate to the girls themselves and to their families the danger they are in. If a captain sees fit to employ force what is to prevent him? Of course, there are lots of captains who are honorable, virtuous men, but it is of the scoundrels that I write and there are lots of them too. The undeniable fact is that no young girl should accept a berth as a cook on a sailing vessel. Mrs. B.

There certainly was some truth to the writer's concerns of safety. As in society in general, unattached females could be open prey. The cooks were usually alone on the ships, without relatives or female companionship. Her cabin was in the deckhouse where the captain and mate slept. The sailors were all forward in the forecastle, perhaps 100 feet distant. In 1880, the cook on the schooner *Jessie McDonald* was reported raped by members of the crew. In 1882, the captain of the schooner *Midland Rover*, in a terrible rage over some slight, fired a gun at the cook. A year later, Mary Linsey, the cook of the barge *Sam Bolton* refused the captains advances so he kicked her "in a brutal manner and put her out on deck for three hours."

There were not enough female cooks to fill all the vacancies in the 1883 Chicago grain fleet. Old ladies were not wanted and farm girls were preferred over city ones. It was said when they left port, at least 50 schooners had "calico cooks" aboard.

Regardless of being a paid member of the crew or a family member, danger still existed. In the summer of 1893, an enterprising Canadian, David John Farrington, purchased the three-masted American schooner *River Side*. The schooner was built in Oswego, New York, in 1870.

The *River Side* was very much of a family business. Sailing with Captain Farrington was his young wife, Annie, acting as cook. She was anxious to do whatever she could to help the new

Regardless of any prejudice, females were frequently cooks on Great Lakes schooners. Stonehouse Collection.

enterprise succeed. Also the adventure of the sailing the lakes was better than sitting at home waiting for her husband to return. Their young baby girl was left in the care of her grandmother.

To help round out the crew, the captain's uncle, Captain Joseph D. Hartgrove, a retired lake master, signed aboard as mate. He also bought his son, John, an experienced sailor. While Captain Farrington certainly was a veteran sailor, having an old hand like his uncle aboard when the fall gales came was a good move.

On October 13, which ominously was a Friday, the schooner left Detroit for Kelleys Island, Ohio, on Lake Erie for stone. There she loaded the heavy slabs of cut stone carefully into her hull, taking time to assure each was adequately secured from shifting in rough water. Two of the crew inexplicably quit the ship at the island. Two more sailors were signed on to replace them, and she hauled off for Tonawanda, New York.

The *River Side* never made Tonawanda. It was said she was seen west of Cleveland, sailing along in easy weather. Then a powerful east gale swept across the lake. When the winds died away, the schooner was gone, wiped away!

Then they found the bottle. Someone hiking the beach near Buffalo found it washing gently in the surf. Inside was a piece of torn brown wrapping paper. Written on it in blunt pencil was the following message: "Whoever finds this please write to Mrs. Jane Farrington, South Side, Ont., that the River Side is full of water and we are all likely to be lost in Lake Erie. Please grandma take care of my baby, for we will all soon be drowned, ANNIE FARRINGTON".

In the spring, Captain W. H. Hartgrove, Captain Hartgrove's brother, went looking for the missing schooner. He thought that they would not have slammed into the gale waves for long, but rather run with the seas until reaching Point Pelee, Ontario. There they would tuck in behind the point and ride out the gale. The old captain's reasoning was solid. Near the Dummy, the wooden beacon marking the east approach to the Pelee Passage, a steamer reported seeing some spars reaching out of the water. Captain Hartgrove put a diver down on the masts, which were in a mere 25 feet of water. He reported the name *River Side* across her stern, but found no bodies. Reportedly only the captain's remains ever washed ashore. The captain's wife had her lake adventure to the misfortune of the families. The young daughter survived until her mid-teens when she died of a lung problem. By cooking on the schooner, Annie accepted all the risks of being a member of the crew, but also the potential of literally wiping out a loving family.

Elizabeth Kennedy was another family cook that met a tragic end. In 1858 the two-masted schooner *Minerva Cook* was sailing off Long Point, Ontario, Lake Erie when she was knocked over on her beam ends during the night in a sudden squall. When dawn broke gray and angry, the schooner had blown to within several hundred yards of the shore. Her masts were pointing inward to the safety of the sandy hills. Monster seas continued to roll over the vessel, then continued on to the empty beach beyond.

Seven people and a big black Newfoundland dog, the captain's pet, hung on to the mainmast, the highest point of the vessel still out of the water. Elizabeth Kennedy, the captain's sister and vessel's cook, was washed off perch three times. Each time the dog Nero dove in and dragged the woman back to the mast where her brother and others pulled her back aboard.

Elizabeth shook uncontrollably and complained of the pervasive cold. The brother stripped to his shirt sleeves to cover her in his own coat. Other crewmen also gave some article of clothing to Elizabeth; maybe a hat, pair of gloves, sweater or scarf. It was plain she was fading fast.

Since she was a timber drougher, the schooner carried two horses forward. They were used both to work cargo and pull the vessel through canals. A small shack near the forecastle served as their barn. When the ship went over, one of the horses drowned immediately. The other, who had been stuck in the shack throughout the long night, finally broke free of the shack shortly after dawn. Confused, the horse started to swim to shore. The captain called him back with a bellowing,"Whoa, Sugar! Come back!" Elizabeth also called after the horse with her weak voice. Nero dove in to the churning water after the horse in an effort to turn him back to the wreck. Incredibly, the horse returned to the schooner.

What happened next is confused, but apparently Elizabeth, Nero and the horse left the *Cook* and headed for the beach. Perhaps Elizabeth slipped into the water again and decided to make a desperate try for the shore. In any case, she was last seen hanging on to the horse's wild mane as the three entered the worst of the breakers. What was even more dangerous was the deadly flotsam in the boiling surf. The schooner's deck load of timber had broken free and could be deadly to a swimmer. The men on the *Cook* couldn't see through the spray if any of the trio had made it to the beach. All they could do was hang on and hope for a miraculous rescue.

Just then, a small fishboat commanded by "Black Saul" Mouck, slipped under the vessel's stern. Black Saul boomed out, "If ye won't jump, I'll come and fetch ye!" He then grabbed a crewman and pulled him bodily into the small boat. Quickly the rest of the crew jumped for it and safely reached the boat. Once aboard they were given blankets and hot whiskey.

When the boat reached the dock the schooner captain asked about his sister. None of the people crowded on the shore knew anything about her. Neither Elizabeth, Nero nor Sugar were seen. They had disappeared in the raging surf. The captain searched the lonely beach for two weeks without finding a trace of his beloved sister. He discovered the horse laying dead in a cedar thicket and the dog high in the dunes. The dog's brains were smashed, perhaps by a piece of timber or by the horse's powerful hoofs. Finally the captain had to return to business. His sorrow could not be forgotten, but life was for the living.

Elizabeth's body was eventually found deep in a cranberry marsh, apparently driven there during the height of the storm. Her hands and face were badly bruised by striking beach stones and floating timber, and her long black hair was tangled with weeds and filled with sand. A gold ring was on her hand.

She was buried where she was found. Moved by the tragedy, a local woman provided a night dress for a shroud. Elizabeth's long hair was so tangled it could not be combed out, so it was cut off and buried with her. A few words from the good book were mumbled over the unfortunate victim, the soil shoveled in and life went on. Word of the find and burial was sent to her brother.

He arrived at the lonely marsh and, after opening the grave, identified his sister by her clothing and the gold ring. The body was brought by wagon to the dock, then carefully loaded on a scow sloop where it was placed on deck and carefully covered with a new sail. The winds blew fair and it was soon carried to Limestone City, Ontario, near Kingston, her hometown. In a mark of mourning, the vessel's bunting flew at half-mast.

But something was forgotten. Next to the empty grave in the cranberry marsh was a small package. In it was Elizabeth's hair. The family didn't know what it was and in their grief they left it on the lonely shore.[26]

THE WRECKED *SLOAN*

On October 30, 1885, a 60-mile-per-hour gale ripped across Lake Ontario, driving the 139-foot schooner *George B. Sloan* into the Oswego, New York, breakwater where she broke up. Only the female cook was lost in the wreck, everyone else was able to scramble up the rocks into safety. Whether the cook was unable to climb over the slippery rocks in her long dress or was just forgotten in the excitement isn't recorded.

The *Oswego Palladium* reported the aftermath: "Yesterday afternoon a diver was busily engaged on the wreck of the schooner *George B. Sloan* and succeeded in obtaining a quantity of the wire rigging, etc. A diligent search was made for the body of the cook, Mrs. Tackaby, but was unsuccessful. Last evening Capt. Scott of the tug *Navagh* found portions of a woman's underwear floating

Sailing the lakes could be dangerous, for men and women. Stonehouse Collection.

outside the piers. It is thought it belonged to the cook of the *Sloan*. A later issue of the paper gave this account of finding the body:

The Body of Mrs. Eliza Tackaby
Drowned on the Schooner *Geo. B. Sloan*
Washed Ashore at Baldwins' Bay

While walking along the beach at Baldwin's Bay, about 10 o'clock yesterday morning, Peter Malott, of the Second Ward, saw floating in the water about twenty-five feet from shore the body of a woman. He called to William Hill, a companion, who was a short distance behind him and together they waded into the ice cold water and brought the body ashore. Coroner Barnes was at once notified and the remains were taken to Dain's undertaking rooms where they were examined by Dr. Kingston and found to be in an advanced state of composition. The scalp was torn from the skull and most of the flesh from the hands. The face was bruised and badly disfigured. The trunk of the body and lower limbs were also badly bruised. The following jury was empaneled, and after viewing the remains they adjourned until 9 A..M. today: A.K. Hill, Albert Place, John Kane, Edward Dowdie, L. Carlton, Frank Ramsdell, John F. Dain, Robert Young, John Matthews.

This morning Captain McDowell, of the ill-fated schooner *George B. Sloan* identified the remains as those of Eliza Tackaby, the cook of the schooner Sloan, who was drowned on the morning of October 30th last, when the vessel went to pieces at the mouth of the harbor. William Hill, one of the men who helped remove the body from the water and formerly sailed with Captain McDowell also identified the remains as those of Eliza Tackaby, cook of the wrecked schooner Sloan

The jury after viewing the remains and hearing the testimony of Captain McDowell, found that the deceased came to her death on the morning of October 30th at the time of the wreck of the schooner *George B. Sloan*, by drowning. The deceased was a widow about forty years of age, and resided in Brighton, Ont., where the remains will be sent to-day for internment. She leaves one son, a young man twenty years of age.

Death at sea! Stonehouse Collection.

At the time of the accident an evening paper stated that Capt. McDowell had offered a reward of $100 for the recovery of the body. "Capt. McDowell said to-day that he did not offer any reward. The finders of the remains feel that they are entitled to some reward, having waded into the lake to rescue the body and then having to carry it through the swamp at the bay to where it could be reached by the ambulance."

"Early this morning a part of the vessel's topmast, eighteen or twenty feet long, washed ashore near Smith & Worts' new box shop in the second ward. It had the appearance of having been broken off recently. A portion of the stay was attached to it."[27]

Another case of shipwreck is that of the 566-ton three-masted schooner *P.C. Sherman*, lost during a November 15, 1871, storm off Lake Erie's Long Point. Captain Charles McMillian abandoned his ship in the lifeboat when her anchors dragged and hold started filling with water. Captain and crew thought they would be able to come ashore on the point, but the wind blew the small boat offshore, where it drifted for 20 hours. When it finally came ashore, it smashed hard against the rocks shattering the hull, and the waves immediately started to swamp the boat. Everyone was numb with cold and covered with ice. All of the crew were able to scramble up the high bluffs to safety, except the woman cook, too numbed to move and weak from hunger. Instead of helping her, the men left her to die. They later claimed they were too weak to help her!

An especially troubling case where a heartless crew left the cook to die occurred on October 16, 1880, when the schooner *J. H. Hartzell* went in the breakers just south of Frankfort, Michigan, on Lake Michigan. The eight-person crew took to the rigging and tied themselves off, as well as the cook, safe from the grasping waves. The cook, Lydia Dale, was sick and unable to fend for herself. When the life-saving crew from Point Betsie arrived, they used their beach apparatus with the lifecar to bring the crew ashore. The lifesavers kept asking for the cook to be put into the lifecar but the crew never did. Each time a man came ashore he said she would be next. Finally all the crew reached the beach. Only the sick cook was left on the wreck. The last man assured the lifesavers the cook was dead. The lifesaving keeper didn't believe the crewman. By then it was too late for the lifesavers to send a man out in the car. It was dark and the mast Lyda was tied to was ready to fall. When dawn broke, the *Hartzell* was gone, smashed into pieces by the storm waves. When the cook's body finally washed ashore, a coroner's jury determined she was alive when the crew left her on the wreck, condemning her to death.

By contrast, extraordinary efforts were sometimes made to save a female cook. After being plummeted by a powerful Lake Ontario storm, the schooner *Cortez* was driven on a sandbar off Oswego, New York, on November 12, 1880. To save themselves from the waves sweeping hard across the deck, the crew climbed into the rigging and lashed off. Before they took care of themselves, however, they dressed the cook in two pair of sailor's trousers and bundled her in a heavy wool blanket, then hoisted her into the ratlines, too! All were saved the next day when a lifeboat reached the ship.

Many women found employment in schooners as cooks. Lake Superior Marine Museum.

Another brave cook who faced shipwreck was Julia Greavreath of the schooner-barge *St. Clair*. On October 1, 1888, the *St. Clair* was anchored off Lake Huron's Harbor Beach, Michigan, trying to ride out a storm. The captain of the steamer pulling the barge had tried to get a tug to go out and tow her behind the breakwater to safety, but none would venture out into the gale whipped lake. The schooner was left to her own anchor to make it through the storm.

About 10:00 p.m., the lookout at the Harbor Beach Life Saving Station saw the *St. Clair* burning a distress signal. Her seams had opened in the heavy seas and her captain wanted his men off now! Keeper George Plough and his crew immediately ran their big 34-foot lifeboat down the ways and rowed out to the schooner. The crew was dressed in warm clothes, oilskins and life jackets. They knew it would be a long and difficult rescue. The crew also gave

Mrs. Plough their valuables to hold for them. No doubt they remembered knew the old lifesaver's motto, "Regulations say we have to go out. They don't say anything about coming back."

When they pulled away from the station dock, Plough knew they would not be able to row back to the boathouse against the force of the northerly waves. Their best hope was to run south with the seas to the mouth of the St. Clair River, 60 miles distant. It would be a terrible trip, but it was also the only salvation!

The big lifeboat had great trouble coming alongside the wildly-pitching schooner but finally, was able to work up to the vessel. Quickly the sailors and woman cook, Julia Greavreath, dropped into the rolling lifeboat. The *St. Clair* foundered a short time later.

It was a wild ride from then on. Plough started his men under oars, but soon set up a reefed sail, steering with the tiller and two quarter oars. Again and again, huge waves threatened to break over the stern, only to rush by either side at the last second. Finally, a monster wave broke cleanly over the stern, carrying away the tiller and almost broaching the lifeboat. Plough then dropped the sail and the men continued under oars.

Throughout the night cold waves swept into the lifeboat, soaking the occupants before flowing out through the freeing ports. One wave flooded out the lantern, preventing Plough from seeing the compass. When the keeper called for matches, only one man had any still dry. The difficulty in relighting the lantern can only be imagined. The constant spray, pitching and rolling boat and numbed fingers made it a nearly impossible task. But finally the flame sputtered to life and Plough swung the lifeboat back on course. Not to have that yellow glow would have been a disaster. There weren't enough matches left to try to relight it.

Just holding the lantern out of the waves that washed aboard was a tough job. Several of the men tried to do it but failed. It was here that Julia, to this point a passenger huddled from the cold in the bow, came forward. In a surprisingly strong voice, she said, "I can do that." She wasn't going to be a passenger any more. She took the lantern and held it firmly throughout the rest of the wild night. She kept the critical lantern burning and gave them all a chance to live.

When the cold light of dawn finally broke, Keeper Plough knew they weren't going to make the St. Clair River. He could see they were barely halfway. They were all exhausted and nearly frozen, especially the captain of the *St. Clair* and Julia. When they arrived off Port Sanilac at about 6:00 a.m., Plough decided their only chance was to attempt a landing there. He would try to run the lifeboat behind the lee of the 500-foot pier and then onto the beach. Word of their epic rescue had preceded them and fully 200 people were waiting on the beach to see the end of the long life or death struggle.

With their last reserves of strength the lifesavers pulled the lifeboat for the pier. Quartering through the breaking seas, they were alternately deep in a trough then balancing high on the tumbling crest. Each desperate minute brought them closer to safety.

Just as the lifeboat reached the end of the pier, a huge wave–a wall of water piled higher by the shoaling bottom–caught the lifeboat and broached it. A quick second wave rolled it completely over, throwing the occupants into the boiling breakers. As designed, the big lifeboat rolled three-quarters back upright, but bottomed out before coming around entirely. Eight of the 16 occupants managed to struggle back into the boat and ride it to shore. Three others swam in to the beach but five people perished, including the brave and courageous Julia Greavreath.

In the 1889 *Annual Report of the U.S. Life-Saving Service*, it was related that "...braver men never manned a lifeboat." However, no mention was made of the critical role played by a humble cook!

Another cook that proved brave in a lifeboat was Ettie Birnie, the daughter of Captain John Birnie. When the schooner *Azov* was overwhelmed by a storm on October 25, 1911, off Lake Huron's Point aux Barques, Michigan, the crew took to the ship's boat. Driven by the northwest wind, Captain Birnie took the small boat all the way across the lake before reaching the safety of the

Canadian shore two days later. Throughout the appalling trip, Ettie encouraged the men to keep on going and not give up. Her father later gave her the credit for keeping heart in them all.

The three-masted schooner *Oliver Mowat* was run down by the big steel steamer *Key West* off Main Duck Island, located just over the Canadian boundary in eastern Lake Ontario, on September 1, 1921. The death of the captain and mate was thought to be caused by their attempt to rescue the cook. After the steamer crashed into the schooner, both men ran below to get the cook, 60-year-old Carrioe McGulgan. None of the three made it topside before the schooner dove for the bottom. Following an investigation, both captain and mate of the *Key West* were jailed for keeping a poor lookout.

Some of the cooks, whether sailors' wives or single women, were hardly classic Gibson girls. A case in point is Mrs. George Mackie of the schooner *James R. Benson*. The canal schooner was upbound on Lake Erie in the summer of 1884. The crew consisted of the captain and cook's husband, George Mackie, two mates, four sailors and the cook.

Mrs. Mackie was a big woman, weighing a solid 200 pounds. One of the crew remembered she was "cheerful as a cricket, an A-1 cook and a mother to us all." She grew up on Garden Island, Lake Ontario. When a little girl fell off a dock in 12 feet of water, she dove right in and saved her. All the men were fooling around with pike poles trying to hook her. Only Mrs. Mackie took immediate action to save the child.

At eight bells (4:00 p.m.,) the mate called the watch below by pounding on the forescuttle and yelling, "turn out, turn out, shake a leg and standby for squalls." The men tumbled out on the rain-swept deck and all hands were put to shortening sail. None of them saw the black squall slam into the old schooner. The deck suddenly tilted under their feet and the men scrambled for their lives.

The ship quickly rolled over on her side with water pouring into the hatches. Loosened sail flapped hard in the wind. When the ship went over, one of the men disappeared in the confusion and was never seen again. Several men ended up on her bow, the rest clinging to the hull. One man saw the cook hanging halfway out of the window in the cabin. Then she fell backwards into the window and vanished from view. Barely a minute later, as the crew watched in amazement, the cook suddenly appeared in the water alongside the schooner. Apparently she had washed right through the mess room and out the cabin door! Two of the men swam out to her and pulled her to the side of the vessel. The men kept rolling and lifting her until she was safe aboard and the water squeezed out of her. One of the men took off his oilskin and covered the shivering woman. She was semi-delirious and sang a hymn all the way through. Then she started to pray and kept at it throughout the experience.

The men had nearly given up hope of rescue, before another schooner, the *Bay Trader*, sighted the hulk. The ship hove to and sent a yawl over to recover the survivors. Much trouble was experienced getting the cook into it, due to her great weight and semiconscious state. When the yawl returned to the *Bay Trader*, there was much trouble hoisting her aboard.

One sailor remembered, "Next morning at seven bells we were called. I went aft and took the wheel and the *Bay Trader* boys went down to breakfast. When they came up one of them relieved me and I went forward and washed with the rest of our crowd and waited for our breakfast call. But no bell rang. The mate of the *Bay Trader* at length went aft and asked the cook if our breakfast wasn't ready yet. {*No,*} said she. {*I was hired here to cook for one crew and that's all I'm going to cook for.*} I have known many lake cooks and most were fine women, but this was a stem winder. She never offered Mrs. Mackie a dry stitch and never said a word to her. Even the captain of the *Bay Trader* was afraid of her, for when the mate reported to him he only said, {*Well, you go and get their breakfast.*} He did."

Female cooks sometimes provided help in difficult situations. An example is provided from the *Oswego Palladium* of July 5,

1878. I am indebted to Mr. Richard Palmer for finding this wonderful material.

> The steamer *Hastings* arrived here about 9 a.m. yesterday with an excursion, most of the party remaining to see the celebration. She left at 10 a.m. with another party of between 300 and 400 people, a large number of whom were from Syracuse, bound for Kingston, and was due here today–and she perhaps never would have arrived here at all except for the favorable circumstances of clear and calm weather, and the fact that there happened to be a woman there who knew more about navigation than anyone else on board. The *Hastings* left Kingston about 5 p.m. When about 15 miles from Oswego, she sighted the light of the N[orthwest] T[ransportation] propeller *City Of Toledo*, bound for Kingston, which left here at 8 p.m. Taking it to be the Oswego light, she followed it back to the Ducks, or thereabouts and at daylight found herself somewhere in the vicinity of Mexico Bay, whereupon she put about and reached here at 7 a.m. From all obtainable accounts, there was no one aboard competent to navigate the steamer and she was finally taken in charge by a woman who ascertained her situation and was practically in command.

Martha Hart, an Oswego woman, who has sailed the lakes as a cook at various periods for the past ten or twelve years, happened to be aboard. Following is her statement to a *Palladium* reporter:

> "We left Kingston at 5:30 p.m.; between 11 and 12 p.m. they spied the light of an upbound N.T. boat and followed her down the lake until they got below the Gallop Islands and about four miles from shore; there they let her lay to the mercy of the waves, had there been any and if there was any at

all they would have been lost; we stayed here till the morning star made it's appearance; the wheelsman point for it; there was no captain, mate nor sailor to be seen all night; he run her for the morning star, running wild until we saw land at Nine Mile Point, about half-past seven; at 2:30 a.m. I told them they were near Sackett's Harbor, below the Galloup and told them to point south and pointed out the direction to Oswego; I made use of marine glasses which I borrowed, the boat's glasses not being good for anything. I told the passengers if they set the table, go for it; but they didn't set any table: we didn't have a bite to eat and couldn't buy it; neither could we even get a bunk to sleep in: the passengers were very much excited and alarmed and anxious to get home."

The statement that no one appeared to be competent to navigate the steamer is corroborated by other passengers. This woman further says that there was no chart aboard. Before or soon after they started to follow the N.T. boat, she saw the Oswego light and pointed it out, but the wheelsman thought he knew better and refused to steer for it. She also relates that when she became satisfied that they were getting dangerously near land, she went down and told the engineer that they would soon be ashore and that he then stopped the engine after which they floated around indiscriminately.

The night was perfectly clear; there was no wind, and there can be nothing but the gravest censure for the exposure of the lives of a large number of people. Oswego families who had relatives aboard spent an anxious night, and the Canadian excursionists who awaited the boat wandered about the streets most of the night. The affair has excited both ridicule and indignation here–ridicule at the inefficiency of the commanding officer of the *Hastings*, and indignation at so dangerous an exposure to human life.

Oswego Palladium, July 10, 1878

The Trip of the *Hastings*

Belleville Ontario:–Both of the Oswego papers have long and sensational accounts of the steamer *Hastings* being lost on the lake, and censure her officers very strongly. We are in a position to say that her officers are not in the least way blamable. On the night in question an old and experienced pilot was placed in charge, in order to relieve the officers of the boat, who had been overworked, and the blame must rest on his shoulders. Either one of the old officers of the boat, under ordinary circumstances, could have taken their boat safely to Oswego.

If a man who cannot tell the Oswego light in a clear and radiant night from the light of an N.T. propeller is considered an experienced pilot for a Canadian boat, the quicker the traveling public find it out the better. Perhaps the Ontario can state what were the extraordinary circumstances under which, on this occasion, either of the old officers of the boat, or both of them could not take their boat safely to Oswego.

Oswego Palladium, July 12, 1878

The Stray Steamer

Kingston News: The pilot [of the *Hastings*] claims that there was a dense fog on the lake during the night, and this was the cause of his following up so closely the lights of the propeller. It is not true

they were within fifteen miles of Oswego. If they had been they could have seen the lights and been all right. Had it not been customary to take a pilot on board to navigate the boat, the officers could have done it easily, as they had both charts and compasses on board. The statements of the Oswego papers are grossly exaggerated, and one of them at least is said to be written in the interest of the opposition boat.

The night of the *Hastings* adventure was perfectly clear, and if there was a fog, nobody but this pilot could see it. The evidence here is that the Oswego light was sighted and pointed out to the pilot, but he refused to believe it, and preferred to trust an N.T. light moving off down the lake. Whether there have been any exaggerations or not, the fact remains, without exaggeration, that a steamer with between 300 and 400 passengers left Kingston for Oswego about 5:00 p.m. could not find the way in a clear, still summer night, floated around in the lake, without her officers knowing where she was, till daylight, and didn't get to Oswego till nearly 8 o'clock the next morning. This is the main and unalterable fact, whatever difference there may be between the officers of the boat and the passengers as to the details. That Oswego papers have an interest in any boat excited a smile here. Oswego newspapers are wealthy, but they haven't any navigation lines that anybody has heard of.

The steamer *Hastings* was 138 feet in length. Originally built as the *Rochester* in 1863, she was owned by Canadian interests at the time of this unusual incident. She went through several alterations and name changes before finally being abandoned in 1914.

———

During the American Civil War Captain William Quick of Presqu'isle Bay on the Canadian shore of Lake Ontario, built a handy little 118-ton schooner he named *Amanda* after his daughter. Amanda was the apple of her father's eye and he spared no effort to make the schooner just as pretty as his little girl. The ship sported a white hull with green trimmings and a red boot top. A half-clipper bow gave her a stylish cut.

Captain Quick often took Amanda sailing with him and under his expert hand she became very handy as a helmsman, although barely able to reach the king spoke when she stood behind the wheel. The schooner would often run with lumber from Dundas, Ontario, for Charlotte, New York. It was a good trade and with captain, five or six men and Amanda, very profitable.

One trip the entire crew jumped ship when they reached Charlotte. At the time it was a common practice. The men would join the Union Army, receive an enlistment bounty, then desert at the first opportunity and either return to the lake or enlist again for another bounty and repeat the entire process. The *Amanda* was not alone in being crewless. Other schooners in port had the same problem. Their captains decided to wait in port with the hope their men would desert quickly and make it back to their ships. Captain Quick said "I have two Amandas," and elected to leave. Some of the other captains gave him a hand hoisting his heavy canvas, then waved farewell.

Quick and his daughter had an easy run across the lake, each taking a trick at the wheel. About mid-lake, Captain Quick sighted a big, foot-square stick of oak, evidently lost overboard from a ship's deckload. He had planned to build another schooner during the winter and name it for his young son, William John. He had earlier built one for Amanda's older sister, Sarah Jane. He decided the timber would make an excellent keel and he would salvage it, even if he only had Amanda to help him. Together the two dropped the gaff topsail and rounded the schooner up alongside the timber. Leaning out he slipped a running bowline around one end of the timber. He ran the rope through a pulley to the windlass and with Amanda's help, heaved the end of the timber high enough to lash it to the rail. They repeated the process with the other end of the timber.

With the prize timber safe aboard, they resumed their trip, alternating steering, sleeping and eating. When they sailed into Presqu'isle Bay the customs officer boarded to determine if there was any American cargo to declare. Captain Quick replied no, only a cargo of Canadian timber. The customs man looked at the captain and asked, "Where are your crew?" Quick pointed at Amanda and proudly said, "That little lass there is all six of them."

————

Cooks sometimes assisted in other ways too. Captain William Malcolm related the story of his daughter Kate, the cook on the schooner *George W. Davis*, who helped him sail through a gale from Rondeau, Ontario, to Buffalo.

Captain Malcolm was at the helm for 18 consecutive hours, while his crew kept steady at the pumps. Kate not only managed to keep the food coming, regardless of the weather, but also was able to spread ashes under her father's feet to give his sea boots traction on the slippery deck. Heavy seas were foaming over the taffrail and one powerful wave swept aboard and smashed the yawl into kindling. Bucking and rolling in the steep seas, the schooner drove on through the hellish storm. It seemed that every few minutes Kate would appear with a dustpan full of fresh ashes, just after the last ones were swept away. When the ashes from the cabin cookstove ran out, she used smashed up lumps of coal. Thanks to the hard work of all, the captain at the wheel, sailors on the pumps and Kate spreading the ashes, the schooner safely made port.

————

There is also the case of a little girl who saved her ship. The old schooner *J. Suffel* was in mid-lake carrying a cargo of coal back to Toronto from Fairhaven, New York, when she suddenly developed an unholy appetite for freshwater. The crew searched as best they could but could not find the leak. The schooner was an old vessel with many hard miles under her keel so it was a risky trip anyway–so chancy in fact that the insurance companies refused to cover her. The ship and cargo were strictly on the owner's account.

It was Captain Stephen Taylor's first trip in the *Suffel* and he brought his young daughter Jessie along both for luck and to act as the cook. Once the flooding started he put her on the wheel, telling her it was a great night for a long steer. She knew nothing of the dire circumstances they were in.

The captain and two men worked the stern pump and the mate and another sailor the forward one. The water kept gaining. Finally, the lee scuppers were level with the lake. There was no doubt that in a short time, perhaps 10 minutes or so, she would plunge. Deciding he had to abandon ship, the captain and another man lowered the yawl while the remainder of the men kept at the pumps. When Jessie asked what was going on, her father gently explained they would be leaving here soon and that they would probably be in the boat for a long time. He suggested she use the head on the schooner before boarding the small yawl.

The men on the schooner always used the "plumbing" over the bows, hanging on to the rigging and shrouds as needed. The lake did a fine job of sluicing away any residual and there was certainly great ventilation. Female cooks always used a slop bucket in their cabin. The *Suffel* however, was rare in that she had an actual toilet in the cabin. This was what Jessie used.

After a couple of minutes Jessie returned to the yawl and prepared to climb over the rail. Before she did, she asked he father, "Why the water was roaring under the toilet like one of those city hydrants bursting?" In a flash her father was down in the cabin and yelling he had found the leak. He sent the crew back to pumping and Jessie to the wheel. The captain then asked for a volunteer to try to plug the hole. One man, an old sailor named Alexander Taylor, no relation to the captain, said he would go, but did ask for a warning if she started to dive while he was below. Opening the aft hatch, the man crawled over the wet coal cargo and just under the cabin floor in a space no higher than perhaps two feet. When he reached the toilet he found the discharge pipe had corroded away from the toilet, providing the opening to the lake. Working alone in the dark, deep under the deck, he managed to stuff some canvas into the hole and spike a couple of boards across to hold it all tight. The effect was immediate. The pumps began to gain.

For 12 long, hard hours the men took turns pumping and steering. Jessie went back to the galley and turned out hot coffee and strength giving chow. The men pumped and ate at the same time! When the ship was finally dry, the men dropped in their places and slept. Jessie went back to the wheel. Two hours later, when she picked up Gibraltar Light, she called the crew.

When the owner discovered what effort was expended on his behalf, he handed Alexander Taylor five, 5 dollar bills then instructed Captain Taylor to have the ship repaired to first class condition and above all else, to double what ever he was paying Jessie![28]

———

The various seaman's unions that periodically sprang up paid little attention to the female cooks. In some instances the women were forced to use the legal system to achieve justice. In 1878, the cook on the tug *Andrew J. Smith* had the ship seized in Detroit to gain payment of $92.50 in back wages.

Women also served as stewardesses, ladie's maids or chamber maids on the passenger steamers, or the rare schooner with passenger quarters.

In at least one instance a woman's traditional sewing work provided the key to identifying a lost vessel. In October, 1880, the schooner *Picton* discovered a mast sticking out of 14 to 15 fathoms of water near the Pennicons, two shoals just outside of the False Duck Islands in Lake Ontario. Wrapped around it was a schooner's fly, staff and all. A fly was a three- or four-yard long bunting cone. The mouth was held open with a hoop and tapered to a small opening at the tail. Every old wind wagon flew one at the maintop masthead and some three-masters had them on the mizzen also.

The men recovered the fly and brought it back with them to South Bay, on the Canadian side of the lake. One schooner was reported recently missing, the *Olive Branch*. The men presented the fly to Mrs. Dix, the missing captain's wife. She had made a new fly for the schooner that summer and she immediately recognized the water soaked hank of cloth as hers. There was no doubt of it. She knew her own stitches![29]

When the schooner *Old Fellow* wrecked at Oswego, New York on October 26, 1876, the cook was the captain's young daughter. She certainly had an experience she did not soon forget. The schooner was bound into Oswego with a full cargo of lumber when she struck the east pier in a gale, losing her bow sprit. Powerful waves drove her down the lakeshore until she hit the shallows just offshore. Her deck load was soon washed away by the seas sweeping aboard and over her open deck. Local residents were able to pass a rope to the men on the schooner and after it was made fast, the stranded sailors were able to come ashore over it, one by one. But not the young cook. A local tug captain, Charles W. Ferris, waded out to the schooner and carried her safely ashore in his arms.

LOUISE CHARTIER

Great Lakes historians have long known of the exploits of Louis Denis La Rhone, the commander of the French post at Chequamegon, in western Lake Superior, from 1727-1741. He is remembered for establishing copper mining and the construction of the first sailing vessels on the lakes. When he died, he was succeeded by his son who held the post in 1741-1742.

What is little-known is that the son was succeeded as commander by his mother, Louise Chartier. She commanded the post for six years. Louise was not a daughter of the frontier. Her father had been a counselor of Louis XIV, and later a lieutenant governor of New France. Louise was accustomed to living in luxury, not in a far-flung outpost in the wilderness. Nonetheless, she adapted to her role and thrived. How much traveling she did as a commander is a mystery, but whatever she did, it had to be on the highway of Lake Superior. Running a far-flung post of New France was very much a "hands on" job! She was the only woman in the history of the New World appointed to the leadership of an important post. She died in Montreal around 1763.[30]

TRAVELERS AND OTHERS

Women certainly shared the danger of working and traveling on the old steamboats. The case of the tug *J.H. Bloore* is a excellent example of a commonplace accident as this newspaper account illustrates.

Oswego Commercial Times, October 18, 1858
Melancholy Accident - Explosion of the Tug *J.H. Bloore*

"This morning about half past five o-clock, the steam tugs *Robert Reid* and *J.H. Bloore* left the harbor on the lookout for vessels on the lake, and when about three quarters of a mile out the *Bloore* burst her boiler. The *Reid* immediately put about, and picked up the Captain, Alonzo Tiffany, floating on the wheel house, with his leg badly hurt and otherwise scalded, and Mrs. Kane supported by a plank, but so badly scalded that her life is despaired of. Her husband, Wm. B. Kane, fireman, is also very much scalded. George Palmer, a deck hand, who was close by the boiler at the time of its explosion, strange to say, was totally uninjured, having been at once precipitated into the hold. Of D. Tremain, the engineer, there has been as yet no trace, though every search has been made. The *Reid* at once brought the sufferers and wreck to shore. The entire inside of the boat is blown clean out, and Mrs. Kane, who was in her berth at the time, was thrown a considerable distance into the lake."[31]

FIRE ON THE *WISCONSIN*

Along with exploding boilers, fire was a hazard faced by every early steamboat traveler. Because of the heavy and unwieldy dresses often worn by women of the period, they were at more of a disadvantage when quick action was needed to escape the flames. The tragedy of the steamer *Wisconsin* in May, 1867, was a case in point.

At about 10:00 p.m. the *Wisconsin* was southbound on Lake Ontario, not far from the St. Lawrence River, heading for Oswego, New York, with roughly 74 people aboard when fire was discovered raging below her boiler. The cry of "fire" was immediately spread among all aboard. The crew reacted quickly but was unable to extinguish the flames and the stern was soon engulfed in fire. Passengers and crew alike were forced to crowd into to the bow. Captain S. Townsend turned his ship for Grenadier Island, off Cape Vincient, and soon her keel slid up on the shelving bottom about 30 yards off shore. Three of her four lifeboats safely brought many of her people ashore. A rope strung between boat and beach allowed others to escape the burning steamer.

In the ensuing early panic, some passengers rushed into one of the lifeboats and attempted to launch it while the steamer was still underway. It quickly swamped and approximately 20 of the occupants drowned. At least six of the people in the boat were women. Encumbered by bulky dresses and sleeping gowns, they were easy prey for the grasping lake.

The *Watertown Daily Reformer* of May 25, 1867, related the sad story of the disaster.

Travel on the old steamers could be palatial, but very dangerous when fire broke out. Stonehouse Collection.

Among the passengers… was a Mr. Chisholm of Canada, on his way to Missouri with his family and goods. When the fire broke out he was sitting on deck, but his wife and children had retired for the night. He called them up hurriedly and sought to safe their lives in a most unfortunate way. One of the small boats was let down to about a foot of the water, and about twenty passengers leaped into it, and Mr. Chisholm assisted his wife, three daughters and a son to get in. One of the frightened crowd cut with a knife the rope which connected the bow of the small boat with the davit, and the loosened end dropped down like a spoon, and at once filled with water. The passengers were thrown out and nearly all drowned. This happened not more than a minute and a half before the steamer struck the shore on Grenadier Island, and had all remained on board, as the Captain ordered, not a life would have been lost.

Mrs. Chisholm, the three daughters, aged respectively twenty, seventeen and fifteen, and the boy of eleven years were all drowned. The father and two older sons, who stuck to the steamer, were saved. Mr. Chisholm had $4,000 in greenbacks, his only fortune, which was in his wife's satchel, and was destroyed in the flames. Thus he was left in a strange land, a widower, bereft of four children, without money or property, with his great grief resting upon his soul, to commence the world anew.

The bodies of his wife and children were recovered and have been interred in the graveyard at Cap Vincent, and the sad, heart-broken husband and father, with his two remaining sons, he will go on to his homeless home in the West. Few life-dramas have sadder chapters than this.

One of the boat's occupants was a Mrs. Gallagher. When the boat was dumped, she caught hold of plank and started to float

Shipwreck on the lakes was commonplace. Stonehouse Collection.

away from the ship. She was only located when the survivors started to search the water for missing passengers.

The local coroner was kept busy. Days after the wreck, he held an inquest "…at the head of Wolfe Island, on the body of a young woman found dead on the beach. She was quite young and well dressed, and was in all probability one of the unfortunate who perished at the burning of the propeller *Wisconsin*."[32, 33]

DEATH ON THE *SEVONA*

Kate Spencer and her friend Lillian Jones were looking forward to their trip. It would be an exciting new adventure for both of them. They were aboard the vessel as guests of the owner, James McBrier, and would receive the best the ship had to offer. Both hailed from Erie and were old family friends of the McBriers. They had made the trip up from Cleveland with the *Sevona* and enjoyed every minute. After the ship arrived in Duluth, Minnesota, to unload her coal cargo there was the inevitable delay waiting for space at the ore dock which gave the women nearly three days to sightsee. Finally, Captain McDonald was notified and the ship shifted across the harbor to Superior, Wisconsin.

When the big steel steamer *Sevona* pulled away from the Allouez docks at West Superior at 6:00 p.m. on September 1, 1905, the promise of a wonderful trip was before them. First it would be the ever changing mosaic of Lake Superior, then through the Soo Locks and on to the lesser lakes. It would be glorious! There were other women aboard, too. Mrs. William Phillipie, the wife of the chief engineer, and Mrs. C. H. (Louise) Cluckey, the cook's wife, were also on for a ride. Louise was naturally helping her husband in the galley. No doubt some of the special meals the women enjoyed on the trip up were due to her "extra" hands.

As a ship the *Sevona* was all they could ask for. Built in West Bay City, Michigan, in 1890, she was launched as the *Emily P.*

The 372-foot Servona was a victim of a Lake Superior storm. Stonehouse Collection.

Weed. At 300 feet in length she was considered large for her day. Originally used in both the package freight and bulk trades, in 1896, she was purchased by James McBrier & Company for use in the Lake Superior iron trade. At this time she was renamed *Sevona*. In February, 1905, she was cut in two and a new 72.5-foot section fitted to her midships to increase capacity.

When the *Sevona* steamed into the open waters of the lake heavy swells were running from the northeast. Otherwise, it was still with no wind or indications of a pending storm. Both Spencer and Jones watched as the hills of Duluth faded into the distance. For a while they did some impromptu target shooting with Captain McDonald. He had purchased a .22 caliber rifle for his son in Duluth and wanted to try it out. The women proved terrible shots while the captain was deadly accurate. When suppertime came both women enjoyed an excellent meal and fine conversation with the captain in the elegant dining room aft. Captain Donald Sutherland McDonald was a veteran master of long experience with many exciting stories to tell. As a youth he was one of only two survivors from a terrible wreck on the Irish coast.

Around 9:00 p.m. both women retired to their forward cabins. They were expecting to be gently lulled to sleep by the steady roll of the big steamer. It was now the weather demons of Superior began to spin their magic. The wind began to blow with marked intensity and soon was screaming at storm force. Huge waves were slamming into the steamer, sending heavy billows high over the pilothouse. The steamer was in the midst of a Superior northerner and fighting for her life. At 2:00 a.m. McDonald estimated he was 70 miles out and an hour past Sand Island, the westernmost of the Apostle Islands. He plainly could not continue to fight his way into the storm. Even the staunch *Sevona* could not handle that kind of pounding. He decided to run back to the Apostle Islands for shelter. Turning the steamer in storm conditions was not an easy thing to do. If he misjudged the waves and the ship was unable to complete the maneuver in time, she would fall into the trough and capsize. After passing the word to his crew, he woke the two women and told them to "put breakable stuff in a secure place as when the boat put about she would toss badly," as Kate Spencer later recalled. Both young women remained in their cabins and dropped back to sleep.

McDonald skillfully turned the steamer and steadied her up on a heading he hoped would bring him to shelter. Without any navigation marks he was running on dead reckoning. For an hour and a half the steamer rode with the waves. The stress was far easier on the ship but McDonald did not know where he was. He woke Spencer and Jones again and instructed them to dress. At 4:15 a.m. he told both to put on life jackets and had four crewmen take them back to the galley. The ship's two lifeboats were aft and McDonald wanted them close by if anything went wrong. Both women had taken care to don their warmest clothing before belting on the heavy canvas life jackets. Two of the sailors held on firmly to each woman. It was a hellish trip for all of them. They had to hold on for their lives to the manila lifeline than ran the length of the open weather deck, as powerful waves doused them waist-deep in water. The wind tore at them, threatening to literally blow them into the lake. All the while only the meager lights from the cabin ports cast any light at all across the dark deck.

Once they reached the aft cabin the two women were hustled into the safety of the dining room. The table was already set for breakfast. When the rolling of the ship threatened to send the dishes flying to the floor, they helped Louise gather them up to secure storage.

The *Sevona* continued on through the storm. In the pilothouse McDonald and his men looked desperately for some sign of where they were. Somewhere in the darkness ahead must be Raspberry or Sand Island Lights. At 5:45 a.m. he guessed he must be near the Apostles and slowed his engines. A bare 15 minutes later the steamer crashed into Sand Island Shoal. The damage was severe. A massive hole was torn in the bow and the ship split in two amidships. The men on the bow were cut off from the lifeboats aft.

The captain used his megaphone to bellow to the chief engineer to lower a boat and put all the women into it, but keep it tied off to the lee of the stern. Kate Spencer remembered: "I cannot think or talk of the wreck without shudder following shudder. At about 6:00 came the terrible crash which broke the vessel in two. We got into the lifeboats at that time but the captain and the other men could not come aft owing to the break. He hailed us through the megaphone, 'Hang on as long as you can.' We did, but the sea was pounding so hard that chief engineer Phillipie finally directed us out of the small boat and into the large vessel again, all congregating in the dining room which was still intact. The big boat was pounding and tossing. Now a piece of deck would go and a portion of the dining room. During all this time the men forward could not get to us."

Captain McDonald put some of the men forward to work building a raft out of the wood hatch covers and cabin doors while others started firing off distress rockets. The whistle blew until the water flooded out the boiler fires. The rockets and whistle went unanswered. At 11:00 a.m. the stern cabin gave every indication of breaking up. The skylight had already been smashed out by breaking waves and water in the room was knee high. Again Kate Spencer remembered, "Everything seemed to be breaking at once and by order of the chief engineer we took to the small boat again. One by one we piled into the boat leaving six men behind us. I never heard such a heart-rendering cry as came from those six. "For God's sake, don't leave us!" they cried. So two of our men got out and helped the six pull the port boat over to the starboard side and launch it. Then we both set out. It was a terrible fight to keep the small boat afloat."

Phillipie took charge of the boat with the four women. To help him he also had his assistant, his son, and three firemen. Deckhand Charles Scouller, who had some small craft experience, took charge of the second boat with five men. The men with the most experience with lifeboats however were in the boat with the captain. Phillipie tried to bring his boat to the bow to get the men there, but the force of the storm prevented it.

The waves grabbed the women's lifeboat and drove it relentlessly to the southwest. Buffeted by the seas, spray flooded into the boat. All the women bailed, constantly sending the water back into the lake. Numbed fingers held hard to tins, buckets and hats as they tried to stay ahead of the relentless waves. For a while it looked like they would be blown ashore on York Island. Instead they scudded by it, unable to reach its safe shores. For a while Louise took a turn at the oars, allowing one of the men to rest. The relentless winds continued to blow the boat over the wildly heaving lake. In the late afternoon the boat reached the mainland but were greeted by cliffs and sharp rocks. Desperately, they all rowed to keep offshore until, finally, Phillipie spotted a small sand beach and headed for it. A large wave picked up the small boat and heaved it ashore. They were safe!

The second boat had a rough time of it until a massive comber deposited it on Sand Island. Almost as soon as the men scrambled out of the boat another wave broke clean on it, shattering it into pieces. They sheltered in an abandoned cabin until a local fisherman found them the following day.

Meanwhile, Phillipie and his four women sheltered as best they could from the storm until a farmer out looking for a pig discovered them and directed the survivors to shelter at a lumberman's cabin. There they were given dry cloths and warm food. With the lumberman as a guide, Phillipie sent out with a horse team to find help for McDonald and the men trapped on the bow. The women rested and recovered in the cabin from their horrible ordeal.

It took Phillipie nearly a day to reach Bayfield. He had to work past nearly 200 windfalls caused by the storm. When he finally reached Bayfield, the storm had decreased enough that he could convince the tug *Harrow* to go out to the wreck. It still took over two hours for the tug to fight through the falling seas to reach Sand Island Shoal. Once they arrived their hopes for the survival of the forward men were dashed. There was nothing left of the bow. It was gone as if it was never there!

Phillipie had expected to find the bow still intact and the captain and crew standing by waiting for rescue. From his vantage point on the stern, the bow looked solid and would survive the storm. He also noticed the captain had both their trunks brought up to the deck as if anticipating a tug and not wanting to discomfort them with their clothing.

The answer to what happened to McDonald and his six men was answered by the Sand Island Lightkeeper, Emanuel Lueck. He had seen the steamer hit the shoal through his powerful marine glasses and watched the rockets arc high into the chaotic sky. He watched as McDonald and his men pushed the wooden raft into the water and climbed aboard. Huge waves overturned the unstable craft and the men climbed back aboard. Time and again the raft tumbled, each time the sailors clawed their way back aboard. The sailors made it all the way to the island's breakers before a huge wave tore it apart and the exhausted men sank into the water. Not one made it to the beach alive! All the while the keeper watched the drama he was helpless to act. He had no telephone or telegraph or other means of signaling for help. His small rowboat could not survive the raging seas and he was alone at the light anyway. There was nothing he could do but bear silent witness to the disaster.

In the days and weeks following the disaster all of the bodies of the sailors were recovered from the Sand Island beach. The discovery of the captain's remains provided a mystery of sorts. He was known to always carry $1,500 on his person to conduct ship's business. When his body was searched, the money was missing although all other personal belongings were in place. It was believed local ghouls had robbed the body of the money. Several local lowlifes were known to be spending unusual amounts of money in the form of battered and water soaked bills in Bayfield bars. Three men were brought to trial. Inexplicably, the prosecutor failed to appear and all charges were dismissed.

Both Kate Spencer and Lillian Jones certainly had an experience they would remember for the rest of their lives. But it was also one they would rather forget![34]

Fire and storm were not the only dangers early travelers faced. Imagine the horror of young Miss Eliza Van Allstine, trapped in the cabin of an upside down schooner! The tale is best told directly from the original:

Oswego County Whig, of July 25, 1838

Shipwreck

The lives of but few persons furnish incidents as appalling as that given below. The account may be in some of the particulars incorrect, as it was penned in a hurried manner, from the lips of one of the sufferers. The new schooner, *William L. Marcy,* Captain Miner, belonging to Messrs. S. & H. Cook, of Ellisburgh, on her trip from Ellis village to Oswego, was on the evening of the 10th inst. capsized in a gale of wind, off Mexico Bay.

The gale was preceded by a dead calm. Upon the first appearance of the storm, every precaution was made use of, to prepare the vessel for its encounter. It is here proper to state that she was without ballast. The progress of the storm could be distinctly traced upon the smooth surface of the water as it came with apparently slow but terrific violence. Its low sepulchral moaning seemed to say to the lookers on, I soon will chant your requiem.

It passed on. With masts perpendicular in the water, and keel in the air, the vessel now dashed to and fro, among the billows. Samuel Cook, (owner) Capt. Miner, and two hands were on deck. William C. Wells, Esq. merchant of Mannsville, John Tift, of Ellisburgh, Miss Eliza Van Allstine of Scriba, Oswego Co. and a son of Mr. Cook, about 12 years of age, were in the cabin.

Those on deck were swept from it as quick as thought; but by such exertions as can only be put forth at such a crisis as this, they all succeeded in gaining the heel, to which they hung from sunset until near midnight, with every sea dashing over them, with tremendous violence.

Little was left of the Servona. Stonehouse Collection.

The cabin filled with water as far as the confined air would permit; the scene which was there
enacted beggars description. Within this narrow 8
by 10 room were four human beings, rolling and

tumbling among the loose furniture and baggage, alternately under and out of the water, as the vessel rose and sunk with each succeeding sea.

They however sustained themselves somewhat by holding on to the inverted berths. After remaining in this situation about two hours with the water gradually gaining upon them, so that but about a foot of space remained between the surface of the water and the top of the cabin, they found to their indescribable horror, that the vital principle of the air was well nigh exhausted.

Death now seemed inevitable. But with a desperation attendant only upon the last effort of the dying Mr. Wells after three or four attempts, by diving down broke out the sky light window and tore out with his hands the iron rods which were placed outside to protect it, through which they thrust as much of the loose rubbish as possible, thereby allowing them room and air, as the water had now free ingress from below. But they still experienced great difficulty in breathing, and must have perished were it not for two feather beds which were inflated with air.

Ever and anon, they thrust these into the water, from which globules of air would rise and burst, thus furnishing a scanty supply of the sustained element. Mr. Tift fainted and sunk but was again brought to the surface of the water by Mr. Wells. The young lady also fainted. The boy sustained himself remarkably. When all hope of relief had fled Mr. Wells with his pocket knife, with no other light than an occasional gleam of lightning reflected by the water, commenced cutting for the purpose of getting a hole through the ship; and had cut through the inner finishings of the cabin and far into the hard timber when his knife came in contact with a spike which dulled it, as to render it useless.

About this time, voices were heard from the outside of the vessel, this being the first sound that had come to their ears, save the howling of the storm, and the peltings of hail upon the bottom of the vessel. the schooner *Pulaski*, Capt. Mathewson, having discovered the wreck, after four hours beating, came alongside and took from the keel the well nigh exhausted sufferers.

But in what way to proceed to rescue those in the cabin, they knew not. While calculating upon the uncertainty of success, Capt. Mathewson formed a quick resolve, and carried into execution the plan which resulted in saving them, and which entitles him not only to their lasting gratitude, but ranks him high on the list of the humanely brave.

With a rope around his body, the waves running fearfully high at the time, he dove under the vessel, and with his feet up felt for the sky light, into which he thrust them, to which they one by one, dove down, caught and were drawn out, with the exception of the boy who was unable to dive as low as the Captain's feet. A hole was immediately cut through the bottom of the vessel, through which he was taken out.

When the hole was cut the discharge of confined air, resembled the letting off of steam, from an engine. No blame is attached to Capt. Miner, he having used every precaution necessary, save a supply of ballast previous to sailing.

EPILOGUE

Women on the lakes as mariners, lightkeepers and other maritime workers, played a role that had essentially two values. As direct participants to the history of the Great Lakes, their contribution was both important yet negligible. There simply weren't enough of them to move the marker in comparison with the males.

However, as trail blazers, as individuals showing the way for future generations, their contributions have been immense. When Celia Parsons ran her boat on Lake Huron she was virtually without contemporaries, a lone woman captain. No matter how well she

Many women yearned for a more active role. Stonehouse Collection.

For most women on the Great Lakes, fishing was not a "sporting" experience.
Stonehouse Collection.

did, there would be few who would immediately follow her. Today, women are commonly deck officers on the big freighters. In some fashion Celia certainly helped show the way.

Whitney and Colfax may have been beacons of sexual equality but they went largely unrecognized as pioneers by society of that time. Perhaps, while it was acknowledged that women could do traditional male things such as lightkeeping, it wasn't seen as something women *should* do. In contrast, women should be wives, mothers, maids, all the customary jobs. After all, there was such a thing as "women's work." It really wasn't until the modern age that the role of women was seen as expanding into the established male domain.

While the suffragettes were effective in eventually getting the vote, they were much less so in changing attitudes about jobs. Women still belonged at home.

When Elizabeth Whitney Williams and Harriet Colfax were tending their lights they were nearly anomalies in the service. While women keepers were not the norm, neither were they

Although often in the background, women worked on schooners, propellers and tugs, as well as waterfront industries that supported the boats. Stonehouse Collection.

unheard of. Both of these women certainly showed that women could successfully keep the lights. As technology changed—specifically the arrival of the big steam fog whistles–it tended to preclude appointing women as keepers, due to the difficulty of hauling the large amounts of coal needed for the signals. Bringing the coal from the boat to the coal pile near the fog house was usually handled by the crew from the tender that delivered it. But moving it to the boilers and removing the ashes was the keeper's job! When the Coast Guard took over the lights in 1939, women keepers, since they were not allowed in the Coast Guard, became more rare. They were only allowed to remain at those lights that required a single keeper. The last woman keeper, Fannie Mae Salter, retired in 1948 from the Turkey Point Lighthouse in the upper Chesapeake Bay in Maryland. Finally, when technology automated the lights and abolished all keepers, women as well as men were eliminated from the position. Job performance was not an issue. Technology, as well as decreasing personnel costs, were the final determinates.

However, by 1942 the Coast Guard had established a women's reserve force which saw extensive duty in World War II, although policy directed their employment in administrative and clerical positions in the continental United States. In September 1944, women were allowed to volunteer for service in Alaska and Hawaii. The women were intended to replace men, releasing them for sea duty or areas closed to women.

Slowly, the gender barriers fell and in April 1979, a female Coast Guard Lieutenant assumed command of the 95-foot Coast Guard Cutter *Cape Newagen* in Hawaii. Others followed. The first woman to command a Coast Guard cutter on the Great Lakes was Lieutenant Sandra L. Stosz, who captained the 140-foot tug *Katmai Bay* from August 10, 1990 to July 24, 1992. At this writing (2000), Lt. Commander Beverly A. Havlik is captain of the 180-foot Coast Guard Buoy tender *Sundew*, homeported in Duluth, Minnesota.

In contrast to young Edith Morgan, forced to watch the heroics of her father and his lifesaving crew from the sidelines, is Inga

The US Coast Guard Cutter Sundew. Stonehouse Collection.

Thorsteinson of the Canadian Coast Guard. Inga demonstrated her courage during the rescue of the crew of the *Grampa Woo*, a 110-foot aluminum "crew boat" used to run summer excursions along Lake Superior's rugged and beautiful shore north of Duluth, Minnesota. At the time of this incident, she was one of just eight women in the Canadian Coast Guard.

On October 30, 1996, the *Grampa Woo* was moored safely in Grand Portage harbor, just north of Duluth. Her propellers had been removed several days before in anticipation of installing new ones prior to sailing to southern waters for the winter. Just after 8:00 a.m. the wind increased dramatically from the west and the *Grampa Woo* began to drag her mooring. Seeing the potential for the trouble, the vessel's two-man crew launched a Zodiac raft and went out to the boat intending to drop her anchor to stop the dragging. When they arrived at the *Grampa Woo*, the raft's outboard engine died and they were only just able to reach the bigger vessel. As they climbed aboard a wind gust blew so hard it picked the Zodiac completely out of the water, snapping the painter securing it to the *Grampa Woo* and sending the raft flying off into storm.

By now the *Grampa Woo* had drifted into water too deep for the anchor to bite and the vessel was headed fast out into the wild open reaches of the lake. The crew could take no action to prevent her from continuing along her deadly course. They immediately radioed for help, but all of the local boats were already out of the water for the winter.

The first effort to save the crew of the vessel was made by the 1,000-foot ore carrier *Walter J. McCarthy*. The big freighter circled the smaller vessel twice but in the heavy seas was unable to get either man safely aboard. The *McCarthy* finally passed a towline to the *Grampa Woo* and made off to the northeast. For nearly six hours the big freighter towed her small charge toward Thunder Bay.

To complete the tow and bring the *Grampa Woo* into port, the 76-foot tug *Glenda* came out of Thunder Bay and sheltered under the lee of Pie Island, approximately 15 miles to the southeast of the

The Canadian Coast Guard motor lifeboat Westfort. Canadian Coast Guard.

city. *Glenda* intended to take the tow from the *McCarthy* off Pie Island when the pair arrived at that location. Bringing *Grampa Woo* into harbor was a job better suited to the tug. The 44-foot Canadian Coast Guard motor lifeboat *Westfort* accompanied the *Glenda*. Inga Thorsteinson was a deckhand on the *Westfort* and a veteran Coast Guardsman. She had braved other storms but this one would be the worst! The west winds were now screaming at 60 knots and seas rolling along at 15 feet. The Canadian Coast Guard 44 boat is very similar to the highly regarded United States Coast Guard 44 boats with the exception of an enclosed pilothouse for improved crew protection. Its twin engines provide 560 horsepower and a top speed of 14 knots. The 3/16 inch steel hull is divided into 9 watertight compartments. The wheelhouse is fully equipped with radar, gps (global positioning system), video plotter, depth sounder, vhf radios and compasses.

When the *Glenda* and *Westfort* reached Pie Island it was approximately 6:00 p.m. and very dark. The 44-foot motor lifeboat, under the command of Chief Coxswain Bob King, was constantly being hammered by the increasing seas. Willie Trognitz was the third crewman. *Westfort* advised *Glenda* by radio that she was close to her limit in withstanding the waves and in fact, waves were coming over her decks and she was taking on water. Both captains agreed to stay in close contact.

Inga came from the Red River area of Manitoba, British Columbia. Growing up around boats on Lake Winnipeg, finding a sea-going career was a natural step for her. Water ran thick in her veins.

Roughly at 7:00 p.m., the towline between the *McCarthy* and *Grampa Woo* broke. The *Grampa Woo* was again at the mercy of the seas. As soon as the *Grampa Woo* broke adrift, both the *Glenda* and *Westfort* headed for her, knowing rescue was now up to them. The *McCarthy* could do no more. The winds now blowing at 70 knots had kicked up 20-foot waves, which punished all three vessels terribly. Pushed by the wind, the *Grampa Woo* was moving eastward at 4.5 knots and both vessels were hard pressed to catch her.

When the *Westfort* turned into the open lake and increased her speed to catch up with the *Glenda*, heavy amounts of water washed onto her deck. Soon the windows and deck were covered in ice. *Westfort* also was rolling up to 80 degrees and the increasingly long recovery time due to the ice build-up on hull and superstructure, was becoming a concern to the crew. *Westfort* was in extremely dangerous conditions. Regardless of the terrible situation, her crew maintained station with the *Glenda*.

The Rescue and Coordination Center in Trenton, Ontario, radioed *Westfort* that she had the authority to leave the scene based on the extreme conditions. The three Coast Guardsmen looked at each other and decided to stay. As the old U.S. Life Saving Service motto went "Regulations say we have to go out. They don't say anything about coming back."

All the crew that sailed on *Westfort* were fully qualified as coxswains and doubtless this helped the motor lifeboat survive the storm. The three constantly rotated between the wheel, radar and lookout astern. The windows were completely iced over and the crew was nearly running blind. In the confused sea, with waves occasionally coming from different directions, each person in the pilothouse depended on the others for survival. Being a woman made no difference. The extreme wave action slammed everyone around the small confines of the wheelhouse equally. Just holding on was difficult.

As the two vessels battled their way to the fast drifting *Grampa Woo*, the storm continued to get worse. Soon the *Glenda's* crew noticed that *Westfort* would provide only an intermittent radar return. Apparently the ice was partly attenuating the radar signal. As the ice built up on the vessel, the *Westfort* became more and more unstable. There was a very real danger she would not make it back to Thunder Bay.

Once the pair reached the *Grampa Woo*, the *Glenda* quickly passed a towline to her. It broke almost immediately. With no other option, the *Glenda* put her bow against the wildly pitching *Grampa Woo* and both men aboard scampered to safety.

*Canadian Coast Guard professional motor lifeboat personnel Ed Greer
and his wife, Inga Thorsteinson. Inga was the heroine (along with two
fellow crew members) of the* Grampa Woo *rescue on Lake Superior.*
Photo by Mauric Gibbs.

When last seen, the abandoned *Grampa Woo* was rolling hard
into the monstrous seas with all lights blazing and drifting fast to the
east. Driven by wind and wave, she finally fetched up on the rocks
of Passage Island, north of Isle Royale, and was battered to pieces.

Both vessels slowly fought their way six long miles back to the protection of Thunder Cape and slipped into the shelter of Tee Harbor on the southeast side of the Sibley Peninsula. Reaching it about 9:00 p.m., they pushed their bows hard on to the gravel shoreline. The freezing spray had knocked out the *Glenda's* short range radar so *Westfort* had to guide her into the harbor. For two nights the *Glenda* and *Westfort* stayed in Tee Harbor, all the while being buffeted by the blasts of the screaming wind. Finally on Friday, November 1, the winds dropped enough for both vessels to make their way back to Thunder Bay. The return was not easy. The seas were running 15 feet high and still very steep and sharp.

In recognition of her role in this heroic rescue, Inga Thorsteinson, as well as every member of the *Westfort's* crew, was decorated for bravery, receiving the "Star of Courage" medal and "Medal of Bravery" from the Governor General. The "Star of Courage" is Canada's highest award for bravery in peace time. Edith Morgan may have had to stay ashore while the lifesavers went out into the storm, but not Inga! As a bit of "role reversal" Inga's husband Ed Greer, a relief coxswain for *Westfort*, waited anxiously ashore by the radio while she was out on the wild lake. How times have changed!

As an after note, the *Westfort's* participation received little immediate attention. In fact, when the crew finally arrived back at the dock, lay off notices were waiting on their desks. The Canadian Coast Guard search and rescue crews are only seasonal employees and the season was ending.

It is fair to say that of the estimated 8,000 shipwrecks on the Great Lakes, probably 7,998 were under the command of men at the time of loss. In 1899, Captain Buckley's schooner wrecked on Lake Huron as we discussed earlier. It took 90 years before another woman lost her boat. When the 180-foot Coast Guard buoy tender *Mesquite* wrecked on Keweenaw Point, Lake Superior, in December 1989, the Officer of the Deck was a female Coast Guard officer. Shipwreck truly knows no gender!

ENDNOTES/FOOTNOTES

1. Adeline Keeling was also frequently identified as Adeline Kieling.

2. There is some confusion about the location. It could be Tawas, Michigan.

3. Elizabeth Whitney Williams, *A Child of the Sea; and Life Among the Mormons*. 1905, pp. 143-144.

4. Mary Louise Clifford and J. Candace Clifford, *Women Who Kept the Lights, An Illustrated History of Female Lighthouse Keepers* (Williamsburg, Virginia: Cypress Communications, 1993), p. 62.

5. Interview, Steve Harold, October 2, 1998.

6. Guy M. Burnham, *The Lake Superior Country in History and in Story* (Ashland, Wisconsin: Paradigm Press, 1996), pp. 358-365; Gregory James Busch, *Lake Huron's Death Ship* (Alpena, Michigan: Busch Oceanographic Equipment Company, 1975), pp. 59-68; *Cleveland Plain Dealer*, October 30, 1922; *Detroit Free Press*, October 23, 1916, July 8, 1917; *Detroit News*, October 11, 1934, May 5, 1938; (C. H. P. Snider, "Schooner Days, CLVIII) *Evening Telegram*; Joseph N. Gores, *Marine Salvage* (Doubleday and Company, 1971), pp.70-71.

7. J. Oliver Curwood, "The Girl Diver on the Great Lakes," *Woman's Home Companion*, 1905.

8. John B. Mansfield. *History of the Great Lakes* (Cleveland: 1899), pp. 468-471.

9. Charles K. Hyde, *The Northern Lights* (Two Peninsula Press: Lansing, 1986), pp. 174-175; William H. Law, *Deeds of Valor by Heroes and Heroines of the Great Water World* (Pohl Printing Company: Detroit, nd), pp 19-20; Laurie Penrose, *A Traveler's Guide to Michigan Lighthouses* (Friede Publications: Davison, Michigan, 1992), p. 52; U.S. Lake Survey, Great Lake Pilot, p. 51.

10. *Annual Report, U.S. Life-Saving Service*, fiscal year 1879. pp. 39-40; List of Great Lakes Life-Saving Station Keepers, Stonehouse Collection.

11. Some sources list the master as Hank Hackett.

12. *Detroit Daily Free Press*, December 3, 1854; Roy F. Fleming, "Abigail Becker, Heroine of Long Point, Lake Erie," *Inland Seas* (October, 1946), pp. 219-223; C.H.J. Snider, "Schooner Days, LXIII, DCCCLXIX, *The Evening Telegram* (Toronto), nd.

13. Bessie Carter, Manistee County Historical Society.

14. *Daily Mining Gazette* (Houghton, Michigan), May 28-30; June 1, 9, 17, 1933, *Fort William Daily Times Journal*, May 29-30, June 2, 1933; "Journal of the Light Station at Rock of Ages Light," May 1933, RG 26, NARA; "Report of Casualty, *George M. Cox*", July 20, 1933, RG 26, NARA; Julius F. Wolff, "A Lake Superior Lifesaver Reminisces." *Inland Seas*, (Summer, 1968).

15. *Oswego Daily Times*, May 3, 6, 1853; *Oswego Daily Journal*, May 1, 3, 1853; Stonehouse files.

16. *Annual Report, U.S. Life-Saving Service, 1914*, pp. 92-93. Stonehouse Files, HOWARD M. HANNA, JR.

17. Linda Grant DePauw, *Seafaring Women* (Boston: Houghton Mifflin Company, 1982), pp. 210-211; Stonehouse Files.

18. C.H.P. Snider, "Schooner Days, CCCXXXIII," *The Evening Telegram*.

19. *Toledo Blade* (Toledo, Ohio), June 18, 1906.

20. *Detroit Free Press*, August 11, 1868.

21. *Detroit Free Press*, July 30, 1903.

22. Phyllis L. Tag and Thomas A. Tag, *The Lighthouse Keepers of Lake* (etc) (Dayton, Ohio: Great Lakes Lighthouse Research), 1998.

23. Mary Richards Gray, "Our Women Lighthouse Keepers," *The Designer Magazine* (1904); *Oswego Palladium*, December 30, 1876; Stonehouse Files; David D. Swayze, *Shipwreck* (Boyne City, Michigan: Harbor House, 1992), p. 112; Thomas S. Thompson, *Thompson's Coast Pilot* (Detroit: Thos. S. Thompson, 1869), p. 49; Elizabeth Whitney Williams, *A Child of the Sea; or Life Among the Mormons* (Elizabeth Whitney Williams, 1905), pp. 140-144, 176-183, 204-209, 212-224.

24. Hans Christian Adamson, *Keepers of the Lights* (New York: Greenberg, 1955), p. 320; *Annual Reports, U.S. Lighthouse Board, 1838-1911*; Mary Louise Clifford and J. Candace Clifford, *Women Who Kept the Lights, An Illustrated History of Female Lighthouse Keepers* (Williamsburg, Virginia: Cypress Communications, 1993), pp. 61-73; Mrs. William H. Harris, *The Old Lighthouse at the End of the Harbor*, 1974, np; "Journal of the Michigan City Lighthouse," various years; Susan Meyer, "A Woman's Place was in the Lighthouse," *Commandant's Bulletin* (47-80), pp. 5-7; "Michigan City File, Office of the Coast Guard Historian: Record Group 26," National Archives and Records Service. Frederick A. Talbot, *Lightships and Lighthouses* (Philadelphia: J.B. Lippencott Co., 1913), pp. 315-316; Thomas S. Thompson, *Thompson's Coast Pilot* (Detroit: Thos. Thompson, 1869).

25. *Logbook of Manitou Island Lighthouse*, October 15, 1885; Stonehouse Files.

26. C. H. P. Snider, "Schooner Days," nd., *Evening Telegram.*

27. David Swayze, *Shipwreck* (Harbor House, Boyne City, Michigan, 1992), p. 219; *Oswego Palladium*, December 3, 7, 1885.

28. C. H. P. Snider, "Schooner Days," CMXXIX, *Evening Telegram.*

29. *Annual Report, U.S. Life-Saving Service, 1889; Chicago Inter-Ocean* April 29, 1883; *Daily News* (Kingston) April 9, 1873; Patrick Folkes, "Cooks and Maids: Women in Sail and Steam on the Great Lakes in the Nineteenth Century," Freshwater, (Spring 1986), pp. 24-30; *Mail* (Toronto) August 22, 1878; *Marine Record*, May 12, 1883; *Oswego Palladium* (New York) July 8, 1878, September 6, 7, 1921; C.H.J. Snider, *Evening Telegram* (Toronto), "Schooner Days," LXXXIV, DLXIV, CXXIII, nd.

30. Guy M. Burnham, *The Lake Superior Country in History and in Story* (Ashland, Wisconsin: Paradigm Press, 1996), pp. 81-84.

31. *Oswego Commercial Times*, October 18, 1858.

32. *British Whig*, May 27, 1867.

33. *British Whig*, May 27, 1867; *Oswego Advertiser and Times*, May 27, 1867; *Watertown Daily Reformer*, May 25, 1867

34. *Ashland Daily Press*, September 5,6, 1905; *Duluth Herald*, September 5,11, 1905; Stonehouse Files.

GLOSSARY

Armored Diving Suit–A diving suit that was essentially made of metal with rubber or canvas seals. It allowed deeper dives than conventional suits.

Beach Apparatus–This term refers to the equipment carried on a lifesaver's two-wheeled cart. Usually it consisted of a line throwing gun (*see* Lyle gun), shot line boxes, sand anchors, hawsers, whip lines, shovels and related items. A life car was sometimes included (*see* life car).

Bends–A form of decompression sickness common to deep-sea divers. It occurs during the ascent or after reaching the surface. It is caused by the transition from higher to lower atmospheric pressure and is caused by the release of nitrogen bubbles which block the blood vessels. It is also called caisson disease.

Boot Top–The part of a vessel immediately adjacent to the waterline.

Bowline–A knot tied in such a way as to make an eye in one end of a rope. A running bowline is bowline made around the main part with the end of a rope and serving as a slip knot.

Brig–A two-masted vessel, squared rigged on both masts.

Bulkhead–A vertical partition which separates different compartments or spaces from one another.

Bunting–Flags or other pendants.

Canvas Patch–A temporary patch used for sealing off hull damage made of heavy canvas.

Clam Bucket–A device for moving bulk cargo. It consists of two scoops like a clam shell, hinged at one point so they can be opened when lowered into a pile of material, but will close when raised.

Daguerreotype–An early photographed produced on a silver or silver-covered copper plate.

Derrick Scow –A vessel fitted with a hoisting apparatus and able to handle cargo without assistance.

Diving Dress –The suit and equipment used by a diver.

Fall–The rope which with the blocks comprise a tackle. The fall has a hauling part and a standing part, the latter being the end fast to the tail of the block. With some, the hauling part is simply the fall.

Flotsam –Floating goods or wreckage.

Fly–A three- or four-yard-long piece of cone-shaped bunting, sometimes used to signal preparation for departure or need for a tug.

Fore castle–The compartment in the bow set aside for living quarters of the seamen.

Fresnel Lens–Lighthouse lens designed and built around a series of glass prisms surrounding a light source in a lenticular configuration. Fresnel lenses were a major improvement over the previous parabolic system, and were made in France.

Grand Army of the Republic (GAR)–An organization of Union Army Civil War veterans.

Helmsman–The man who steers, the quartermaster.

Hoop Skirt–A woman's skirt stiffened with hoops.

Hurricane Deck–An upper deck above the superstructure. Often used as a promenade deck on passenger vessels.

Lamproom–Upper room on a light tower where the illuminating apparatus was located.

Lewis Equipment–The term applies to a complicated arrangement of lenses and lamps developed by Winslow Lewis for use in early U.S. lighthouses.

Lifecar–A small metal boat with covered decks that was used by the U.S. Life Saving Service to rescue victims from shipwrecks. Access was provided through a deck hatch and it could carry up to four people within its tight confines. It was employed in place of the breeches buoy.

Lifeboat–There are two meanings to the word. First, it is a generic term for any small rowing boat carried on a vessel for the crew and passengers to escape in, should the ship sink. It is also applied to a very special type of rowing boat used by the U.S. Life Saving Service.

Lusitania–British liner torpedoed on May 7, 1917 by German submarine off the Irish coast. The liner was attempting to run the German blockade when the incident occurred.

Lyle Gun–Small line throwing gun used by the U.S. Life Saving Service.

Mass Copper–A term applied to any large piece of solid native copper.

Mizzen Boom Topping Lift–A rope device used to raise and secure the mizzen boom. The mizzen was the aftermost mast and the boom the wood spar used in conjunction with the mast and sail.

Oilskins–Foul weather gear, cotton garments waterproofed by repeated coats of linseed oil.

Painter–A rope in the bow of a boat for towing or making fast.

Pierhead–The projecting or offshore end of a pier or jetty.

Polygamy–Marriage to more than one spouse.

Punt–A small flat-bottomed boat.

Rigging–The ropes of a ship. The rope supporting the spars is called standing rigging and the ropes used in setting and furling sail are known as running rigging.

Schooner–Fore- and aft-rigged vessel of any practical number of masts above one.

Scow Sloop–A single-masted sailing vessel of light draft used in the local transportation of goods.

Shrouds–Pieces of rope fitted over the mastheads. They are made fast to turnbuckles or deadeyes and lanyards to the chain plates at the vessel's sides. They stay a mast at its sides.

Spar–A general term for a piece of round timber used for masts, booms, gaffs, bowsprits, etc.

Steamboat Inspection Service–A bureau of the Department of Commerce with the responsibility of safeguarding the lives of passengers on steamboats and other vessels engaged in marine transportation. The bureau was handle machinery and hull inspection, licensing officers and conducting trails and investigations as required.

Stove–A vessel broken in from the outside.

Timber Drouger–A bluff modeled sailing vessel engaged in hauling timber cargoes.

Thole Pin–Wooded pins that fit up in the rail of a boat to hold the oars in place while rowing.

Topsail yards–The spar crossing a mast horizontally from which the topsail is set.

Weather Earing–A short piece of rope secured to the grommet of a sail for hauling out the sail to its proper yard, gaff or boom when bending on or reefing.

Whip Line–A rope used by the U.S. Life Saving Service when rigging a breeches buoy.

Wind Wagon–An old term for any wind-powered vessel.

Victorian Era–The art, taste, thoughts and style prevalent during the reign of Britain's Queen Victoria, 1837-1901.

Volunteer Infantry Regiment–A military unit raised during the American Civil War.

Yawl Boat–A square -sterned wooden work boat, often carried at the stern of sailing vessels.

Wrecking Captain–The master of a salvage vessel.

Wrecking Jacks–Large jacks used in removing wrecked vessels.

BIBLIOGRAPHY

BOOKS

Adamson, Hans Christian. *Keepers of the Lights*. New York: Greenberg, 1935.

Burnham, Guy M. *The Lake Superior Country in History and in Story*. Ashland, Wisconsin: Paradigm Press, 1996.

Busch, James Gregory. *Lake Huron's Death Ship*. Alpena, Michigan: Busch Oceanographic Equipment Company, 1973.

Clifford, Mary Louise and J. Candace. *Women Who Kept the Lights, An Illustrated History of Female Lighthouse Keepers*. Williamsburg, Virginia: Cypress Communications, 1933.

DePauw, Linda Grant. *Seafaring Women*. Boston: Houghton Mifflin Company, 1982.

Harris, William H. *The Old Lighthouse at the End of the Harbor*. 1974.

Hyde, Charles K. *The Northern Lights*. Lansing, Michigan: Two Peninsulas Press, 1986.

Johnson, Robert Edwin. *Guardians of the Sea, the History of the U. S. Coast Guard, 1915 to the Present*. Annapolis, Maryland: U.S. Naval Institute Press, 1987.

Law, William H. *Deeds of Valor by Heroes and Heroines of the Great Water World*. Detroit: Pohl Publishing Company, nd.

Mansfield, John B. *History of the Great Lakes.* Cleveland, Ohio: J.H. Beers, 1899.

Neidecker, Betty. *The Marblehead Lighthouse.* 1995.

Penrose, Laurie. *A Traveler's Guide to Michigan Lighthouses.* Davison, Michigan: Friede Publications, 1952.

Swayze, David. *Shipwreck.* Boyne City, Michigan: Harbor House, 1992.

Tag, Phyllis L. and Tag, Thomas A. *The Lightkeepers of Lake Erie.* Dayton, Ohio: Great Lakes Lighthouse Research, 1998.

—*The Lightkeepers of Lake Huron*

—*The Lightkeepers of Lake Michigan*

—*The Lightkeepers of Lake Ontario*

—*The Lightkeepers of Lake Superior*

Talbot, Frederick A. *Lightships and Lighthouses.* Philadelphia, J.B. Lippencott Company, 1913.

Thompson, Thomas S. *Thompson's Coast Pilot.* Detroit: Thos. S. Thompson, 1869.

Williams, Elizabeth Whitney. *A Child of the Sea; Or Life Among the Mormons.* Elizabeth Whitney Williams, 1905.

PERIODICALS

Coast Guard Bulletin. 1948.

Curwood, J. Oliver. "The Girl Diver of the Great Lakes," *Woman's Home Companion*, 1905.

Fleming, Roy F. "Abigail Becker, Heroine of Long Point," *Inland Seas*, October, 1946.

Gray, Mary Richards. "Our Women Lighthouse Keepers," *The Designer Magazine*, 1904.

Meyer, Susan. "A Woman's Place is in the Lighthouse," *Commandant's Bulletin*.

Wolff, Dr. Julius F. Jr. "A Lake Superior Lifesaver Reminisces," *Inland Seas*, Summer, 1968.

NEWSPAPERS

Ashland Daily Press (Ashland, Wisconsin), September5, 6, 1905.

British Whig (Kingston, Ontario), May 27, 1867.

Cleveland Plain Dealer (Cleveland, Ohio), October 30, 1922.

Daily Mining Gazette (Houghton, Michigan), May 28-30, June 1, 9, 17, 1933.

Detroit Free Press, December 3, 1854; August 11, 1868; July 30, 1903; October 23, 1916.

Detroit News, October 11, 1934.

Duluth Herald (Duluth, Minnesota), September 5, 11, 1905.

Evening Telegram (Toronto, Ontario), C.H.J. Snider Column, LXIII, CLVIII, CCCXXXIII, DCCCLXIX, nd.

Fort William Daily Times Journal (Fort William, Ontario), May 29-30, June 2, 1933.

Oswego Advertiser and Times (Oswego, New York), May 27, 1867; August 14, 1868..

Oswego Commercial Times (Oswego, New York), October 18, 1858.

Oswego County Whig (Oswego, New York), July 25, 1838.

Gray, Mary Richards. "Our Women Lighthouse Keepers," *The Designer Magazine*, 1904.

Meyer, Susan. "A Woman's Place is in the Lighthouse," *Commandant's Bulletin*.

Wolff, Dr. Julius F. Jr. "A Lake Superior Lifesaver Reminisces," *Inland Seas*, Summer, 1968.

NEWSPAPERS

Ashland Daily Press (Ashland, Wisconsin), September5, 6, 1905.

British Whig (Kingston, Ontario), May 27, 1867.

Cleveland Plain Dealer (Cleveland, Ohio), October 30, 1922.

Daily Mining Gazette (Houghton, Michigan), May 28-30, June 1, 9, 17, 1933.

Detroit Free Press, December 3, 1854; August 11, 1868; July 30, 1903; October 23, 1916.

Detroit News, October 11, 1934.

Duluth Herald (Duluth, Minnesota), September 5, 11, 1905.

Evening Telegram (Toronto, Ontario), C.H.J. Snider Column, LXIII, CLVIII, CCCXXXIII, DCCCLXIX, nd.

Fort William Daily Times Journal (Fort William, Ontario), May 29-30, June 2, 1933.

Oswego Advertiser and Times (Oswego, New York), May 27, 1867; August 14, 1868..

Oswego Commercial Times (Oswego, New York), October 18, 1858.

Oswego County Whig (Oswego, New York), July 25, 1838.

Oswego Daily Journal (Oswego, New York), May 1,13, 1853.

Oswego Daily Times (Oswego, New York), May 3,6, 1853.

Oswego Palladium (Oswego, New York), May 1, 1865, October 27, December 30, 1876.

Toledo Blade (Toledo, Ohio), June 18, 1906.

Watertown Daily Reformer (Watertown, New York), May 25, 1867.

GOVERNMENT DOCUMENTS

Annual Report of the U.S. Life-Saving Service, Fiscal Year 1879. Washington, DC: U.S. Treasury Department, 1880; 1914.

Annual Reports of the U.S. Lighthouse Board, 1838-1911, Washington, DC: U.S. Treasury Department.

Great Lakes Pilot. U.S. Lake Survey, 1955.

"Journal of the Lighthouse at Manitou Island, Lake Superior," October 15, 1885, NARA, RG 26.

"Journal of the Light Station at Rock of Ages," National Archives and Records Administration (NARA), Record Group (RG) 26.

"Journal of the Michigan City Lighthouse," various years, NARA, RG 26.

"Report of Casualty, *George M. Cox*," July 20, 1933, NARA, RG 26.

"Michigan City File," Office of the U.S. Coast Guard Historian, Washington, DC.

INTERVIEW

Interview, Inga Thorsteinson, September 22, 2000.